NATIONAL BANK
OF COMMERCE
1873-1993

NATIONAL BANK OF COMMERCE

THE FIRST 120 YEARS

BY DR. CHARLES W. CRAWFORD

Memphis, Tennessee

Published by National Commerce Bancorporation
Designed by Jay and Lisa Jo Perdue, Perdue Creative
Copyright © 1993 National Commerce Bancorporation

DEDICATION

To the family of National Commerce Bancorporation
directors, officers, and employees, and to the communities they serve.

TABLE OF CONTENTS

"The past is but the beginning of a beginning, and all that is and has been is but the twilight of the dawn..."
Herbert George Wells, 1866-1946

FOREWORD

BY BRUCE E. CAMPBELL, JR.
CHAIRMAN OF THE BOARD
APRIL 1, 1993

There are many reasons why people reflect on the past and record the events which make up history. Chief among these is, hopefully, to see the present more clearly, to understand more fully who we are today, and to know where we might be heading tomorrow. But there is also the longing to know and understand the past.

It is significant to record the history of National Bank of Commerce now. Today is a milestone marking our 120th anniversary. It has been nearly four decades since we last paused to have a written history of the company. It seemed important to capture, firsthand, the fresh recollections of some of the bank's directors and key supporters. Prominent businessmen and contributors to both the company and the city's development, Robert G. Snowden, Walter P. Armstrong, Jr., Benjamin Goodman, John D. Canale, Jr., W. Neely Mallory, Jr., Lucius E. Burch, Jr., Rudi E. Scheidt, Wayne W. Pyeatt, and others were generous in their time to provide their personal insights and reflections. While documents and events capture the facts of our heritage, it is individuals such as these who put the flavor and character of the past in personal perspective.

Dr. Charles W. Crawford has done a fine job of documenting and compiling the information presented here. Equipped with the expertise of both an historian and an author, Dr. Crawford has assembled the facts of our company's history and put them together with the intangibles that define the institution's personality. His hours and months of research, interviews, writing, and editing have resulted in a book that captures the heritage of our company. He has taken the journalistic facts of now-yellowed newspaper articles, the records and deeds of a business institution, and the memories of the company's friends and associates, and composed the story of our first 120 years. I would be remiss if I did not single out for special thanks M.J. "Jekka" Ashman, vice president. She has acted as coordinator of this project and, apart from Dr. Crawford, is the one most responsible for its satisfactory completion.

In my 26 years with the company, the banking industry has changed a great deal. But the one thing that has not changed, throughout our history, and will not change in the future, is the quality of our people. I honestly feel that the people of our company are exceptional. We would all agree they are our greatest asset. It is appropriate that I, speaking for myself and for the company's stockholders and friends, express thanks to all of them for their good work and diligence. I also wish to thank the Board of Directors for their years of unswerving and solid support during my years as Chairman, and before. As this book attests, they have been of wonderful encouragement and support to me and our management in good and tough times.

In closing, we look now to the future and to where we are headed. No one of us is smart enough to know what lies ahead, to know the shape of the industry in the future, but our people are our best hope for continuing performance in the future as in the past. The National Bank of Commerce family of managers, employees, and directors looks forward confidently to continuing in this, the beginning of our next 120 years.

INTRODUCTION

BY LUCIUS E. BURCH, JR.
PARTNER: BURCH, PORTER & JOHNSON
ATTORNEYS AT LAW

The autumn of 1917 was an exciting time. The world was at war, and even a little boy, five years old, living on a farm near Nashville, did not miss the excitement. My father was at Ft. McClellan preparing his hospital unit for service on the Western Front. My dearly beloved cousin, Lucia, the daughter of my Uncle Charles, who lived in Memphis, was getting married to Lt. Thomas Wood Vinton, whose father was the president of the Bank of Commerce and Trust Company, known today as National Bank of Commerce. It was a big occasion in my family and would have been so in any event, but with the knowledge that the war might scatter us all about in the times to come, great preparation was made for the wedding. My mother had convinced herself that I was a beautiful child and had steadfastly refused to cut my long, golden locks which came down to my shoulders. I had a part in the wedding as ring bearer, flower girl, or something that required me to march down the whole length of the church aisle. I hated every minute of it!

Mr. Thomas Vinton, the president of the bank, a very kind and understanding man, tried to devise some entertainment for me. He took me to the bank building after hours and down into the dark vault. There he touched a wire and immediately two guards, in uniform with pistols drawn, came tearing down the steps. I thought it was the finest thing I had ever seen, and I have had a love affair with National Bank of Commerce ever since.

My father returned from France as did young Lt. Vinton, with the Distinguished Service Cross and two Purple Hearts, and throughout the country some measure of normalcy was restored. It was not to last for long. It was a period of expansion, of playing catch-up at first, but cycles are hard to gauge and what was expansion became over-expansion on a national scale. When the inevitable deflation occurred, no bank escaped. Every national bank in the country was closed and instead of currency, goods and services were paid for with fiat money or "script" until the panic

began to abate. Many of the region's strongest banks closed never to reopen, or were merged into stronger banks. National Bank of Commerce was not without its troubles, largely caused by the debt incurred in the construction of its new building at Second Street and Monroe Avenue, but because of the loyalty of depositors and the ability of its directors and officers, the bank emerged stronger than before.

I came to Memphis to practice law with my Uncle Charles in 1936 and my relationship with the bank has been active ever since as a depositor, borrower, director, and attorney.

Every successful corporation has a character. NBC has one that is distinct and identifiable. Though reasonable minds might differ as to why this is so, I believe it is because so many of the directors and officers have, personally or through their families, agrarian backgrounds. The bank has, over the years, been the bank of choice of those in the cotton business, plantation owners, factors, and merchants. This is certainly

5

not true in every case, nor is the reason as compelling now as it once was, but a generation ago the directors, as directors always have and always will, tried to get men on the board whom they perceived as having the same values and ethics as their own. This has resulted in a board and officers who are conservative; mostly agreeable in business, social, and political matters; and who respect and trust and generally like each other.

I joined the board in 1976, which was during the last period of turmoil that has beset the bank. The formation of the former holding company, United Tennessee Bancshares Corporation (UTBC), which included five separate banks, each with its own board and officers, was a great mistake and soon recognized. Members of bank boards are generally strong-minded people with well developed egos and opinions, and the lack of harmony soon made it clear that the marriage had been a misjudgment and that a divorce was needed. Indeed, I was placed on the board at the urging of Calvin Houghland of Nashville, a major stockholder of Nashville City Bank, and I like to think I rendered some small service in bringing about a friendly dissolution. Since the formation of National Commerce Bancorporation (NCBC), which owns 100 percent of the stock of all of its constituent companies, the nature of the old Board of Directors of National Bank of Commerce has reasserted itself, and congeniality and trust has existed to such a degree that I cannot remember a single incident causing a serious disagreement. Where there has been any disagreement, it has always been resolved quickly to the full satisfaction of all concerned.

Perhaps the greatest contribution to the success of the bank has been the presence of its chief officers, Bruce E. Campbell, Jr., chief executive officer, and Thomas M. Garrott, president. It is impossible to praise these men too highly. They are different types, but their strengths are complementary.

Bruce Campbell has been a banker all of his adult life. He became chief executive officer when Wayne W. Pyeatt resigned amid the confusion and aftermath of the UTBC holding company struggle. Campbell is a "banker's banker," cool, highly intelligent, conservative, a man who takes the long view, and a firm believer in adherence to plans and budgets. His leadership has been largely responsible for the development of a corporate culture that has guided the bank to its present eminence in the industry.

Tom Garrott comes from a different discipline, the wholesale grocery business. He brought to the bank experience in operating on very low margins, highly sensitive to the need for productively employing capital, and in marketing. He was influential in forming the decision to sell the bank's downtown properties with a lease-back option, thereby making more productive use of capital, and in the decision to branch into supermarket banking, providing easily accessible banking service without the high capital cost in brick and mortar, an idea which has been widely sold to other banks under NCBC licensing agreements.

They have functioned as a team, each respecting and using the strengths of the other, and the board has been very farsighted in insuring that both will be available at least until 1996. I cannot imagine a better board with better officers, but it is easy for anyone with a pleasant relationship with any person or group to be subjective in his judgment — indeed, it is hard not to be, but my opinion will withstand the most objective testing, for example:

In 1992, Thomson BankWatch, Inc., a highly regarded rating agency exclusively monitoring financial institutions, rated the overall quality of NCBC "A." This rating is the highest given by Thomson BankWatch, whose analysts follow more than 500 financial companies.

In its 1992 survey of 144 of the nation's largest bank holding companies, financial industry investment specialists Keefe, Bruyette & Woods, Inc. (KBW) ranked NCBC second in compound growth in earnings per share, placing the company among an elite group of only eight bank holding companies in the survey that had suffered no year-to-year declines in earnings per share since 1980. This marked NCBC's fifth consecutive year to be named to KBW's prestigious "Honor Roll."

Alex. Brown & Sons, Inc. said in its January 1992 "Bank & Thrift Group" report, "...not all banks are languishing along with the economy. One bank that keeps churning out superior returns while maintaining a pristine balance sheet is Memphis-based National Commerce Bancorporation."

In its April 1992 issue, *U. S. Banker* ranked NCBC 22nd among the magazine's list of the nation's 60 most profitable banks. The ranking was based on average adjusted return on assets for the 1988 to 1991 period.

Chronicling NCBC's success in supermarket banking, the August 3, 1992, issue of *Forbes* called the company "the country's fourth most profitable bank."

Today, NCBC would be an attractive target for acquisition by a large bank wishing to establish a presence in Tennessee. Under the Clinton Administration, it is a good bet that interstate banking will be easier to accomplish than formerly, but here again, NCBC is in a most comfortable position. It will never need to seek a "white knight" or fear a "black knight," or to adopt a "poison-pill" defense, because 47 percent of its entire outstanding stock is owned by officers, directors, managers, employees, and its pension, trust, and retirement funds. It has not the slightest need to fear abduction, and if it is ever acquired, it will be by an entity with ample funds and the fullest recognition of the extraordinary attractiveness of the bank, and ready to pay for it.

The only fear that I have is complacency. Things are too good and the future does not disclose any great causes of worry. It would be very wrong, though, to assume that all the dragons have been slain. They will always be somewhere, ready to come charging out at the most unexpected times and from unexpected places. As to those future battles, one can only say with Alfred Edward Housman, who on the occasion of Queen Victoria's Jubilee charged his countrymen:

"Get you the sons your fathers got, and God will save the Queen!"

The first home of the Bank of Commerce was 12 Madison Avenue, one of the most magnificent buildings in the Memphis business district.

CHAPTER ONE

THE FOUNDING
OF THE BANK OF COMMERCE

On Monday, April 1, 1873, an event of great significance for the future of Memphis, Tennessee, took place. A new financial institution, the Bank of Commerce, opened for business. The formation of this institution was a product of the era, the region in which it was founded, and, most of all, the vision and organizational talent of the men who joined to create it. They were: Edgar McDavitt, Robert A. Parker, Thomas H. Allen, F. McDavitt, J. T. Fargason, Howell E. Jackson, Nathan Adams, Oliver Hazard Perry Piper, and Eugene Magevney.

Newspaper notices were immediately placed to announce the opening. They informed readers that: "The managers of this bank take pleasure in notifying the general public that it is now open for business, and the accounts of individuals and corporations are respectfully solicited. Prompt and careful attention will be paid to all collections in this and other cities."

Although the bank officially opened to the public in April, the formal meeting of organization had obviously been held earlier. According to an article in the Memphis *Daily Avalanche*, the founders had apparently held a meeting for this purpose on Thursday, March 28. At this meeting, the officers gave final approval to the formal details of opening the bank.

Planning and preparation had probably begun at least as early as 1872, because even in the late 19th century, organizing and opening a major financial institution was a complex venture. One of the most magnificent buildings in the business district of the city had been acquired, furnishings and equipment had been installed, and a substantial capitalization of $200,000 had been raised.

While this amount of capital may not seem impressive a century and a quarter later, following more than 100 years of currency inflation, it was an unusually strong capitalization for a Southern bank in the early 1870s. According to the *Merchant's and Banker's Register*, published by *Bankers Magazine of New York* during the previous decade, only one of the eight banks in Memphis at that time had a capitalization in excess of this amount.

At its founding, as in subsequent years, the greatest assets of the Bank of Commerce were the character, reputation, and business judgment of its leaders. Although each had unique experiences in life, they had much in common. All were men who had achieved business and financial success during the troubled times through which their city had developed. They had lived through the vicissitudes of business boom and depression, Civil War and Reconstruction, followed by renewed growth and expansion. Their names, like those of officers and directors of the other banks of the city in all eras of its history, were associated with the major economic enterprises of Memphis. Politicians, military officers, religious exhorters, intellectuals, and reformers have achieved recognition at different times in the history of the city, but the men who have always provided its consistency of leadership and direction have been those who managed its dominant financial institutions. They were referred to in a much later article in the *New York Times* as the "business oligarchy" of Memphis. It is an appropriate description of the men who met in 1873 to establish the Bank of Commerce.

Edgar McDavitt was born in 1806, during the administration of United States President Thomas Jefferson, 13 years before the founding of the city of Memphis. In 1844, at the age of 38, he moved from Shelby County, Kentucky, to Memphis in Shelby County, Tennessee, to begin a career in business. During this decade, when the population of the city quadrupled from less than 2,000 to more than 8,000, there was adequate opportunity for men seeking positions in growing businesses. He served with increasing success for the next eight years in the firm of Stratton, Goodlett & Company.

Edgar McDavitt

In 1852, the firm became Stratton, McDavitt & Company, and Edgar McDavitt's stature in the Memphis business community increased. During the decade of the 1850s, when the population of the city almost tripled in size, he became a successful financier as well as a leading wholesale merchant. The respect the citizens of his adopted city had for him is indicated by the fact that he was elected to four different terms as a member of the Memphis Board of Aldermen during the turbulent decade of the 1850s. He resigned from the board during two of these terms, but that was not unusual for the time. Twenty-two resignations took place at one time or another from the Memphis Board

of Aldermen during the 1850s.

When the Civil War began in April 1861, Edgar McDavitt was a supporter of the Confederate cause. Fifty-five years of age at the time, he was too old to enter military service. Many of his business friends enlisted in the Confederate army, as did others he had known in community and political service, including Nathan Bedford Forrest who became one of the most successful generals on either side during the war.

Following the destruction of the Confederate River Defense Fleet during the epic Battle of Memphis on June 6, 1862, the city was surrendered to the Union army. Viewed by most of the municipal residents, this encounter was the greatest battle fought by river gunboats during the Civil War, and probably the largest in history. Edgar McDavitt may have been among the spectators. Federal occupation brought disaster to his business operations. The firm of Stratton, McDavitt & Company failed soon after the surrender of the city. Memphis remained under federal military occupation until the end of the war. The success of the firm had been built on an extensive trade with the Mid-South area served by the city, and the production and trade in cotton was disrupted by military operations. Since most of the area around Memphis remained loyal to the Confederacy, the trade with this hinterland was forbidden by the Union military commanders in the city. A limited amount of smuggling took place and some lucrative trading in cotton was done by army officers and their associates, but businesses owned by Confederate sympathizers were given none of these opportunities.

While it is likely that McDavitt managed to save some of his various assets after the collapse of Stratton, McDavitt & Company, it is certain that he retained his business acumen and the respect he enjoyed in the community. His firm was reorganized following the end of the war as Stratton, Goyer & Company, but if McDavitt had any interest in this new organization, it appears to have been a minor one. He continued his business activities during the Reconstruction era and served as financial agent of Memphis during the administration of Mayor J. E. Leftwich during 1868-1869. He was also selected as president of the Merchants Insurance Company, which position he held when plans for the Bank of Commerce began to be made.

The other member with the same family name, F. McDavitt, who was listed in newspaper notices as one of the directors of the bank in April 1873, was apparently a relative of Edgar McDavitt. No other information is available about him, although several members of the family were active in merchandising and the cotton business in Memphis during this era.

Considerably more information is available about another principal founder of the Bank of Commerce, Robert A. Parker, Jr. During the 92 years of his life, he grew up as the city of Memphis did and lived through the first 55 years of the existence of the bank. Born at Somerville, Tennessee, in 1836, he moved to Memphis with his parents in 1841. The population of the city at that time was only about 2,000, concentrated mainly in the blocks between Main Street and the Mississippi River. The streets, although surveyed along their present lines, were roads of dirt in dry weather and mud during rains. All were unpaved and had been cleared of trees and stumps for less than two decades. Hardwood forests and scattered farms filled what is now the remainder of the urban area and wild animals still roamed near the residences of the settlers.

His father, Robert A. Parker, Sr., built a white frame cottage at the intersection of two of these dirt roads, Main and Madison. Young Parker later reminisced about growing up in this home at the edge of the city, playing leap frog on Main Street and pretending to hunt bears and Indians in a gully near the location where Main Street and Monroe Avenue were later graded and paved. His father took full advantage of his contacts in the rich plantation area of Haywood County where he had previously lived. Opening a successful cotton business, he rapidly prospered to the extent that six years later he built a 23-room colonial-style mansion on South Third Street at Maryland Avenue. This well constructed home stood as a landmark in downtown Memphis for more than a century.

It was in this home that young Parker grew to manhood and from it in 1861, at the age of 25, he joined his two brothers to walk the short distance to Court Square where they were mustered into the Confederate army. He served as a soldier in the Army of Tennessee through the Civil War. By 1864 he had been promoted to captain and commanded an artillery battery in the defense of Atlanta. For the remainder of his life, he was known to his friends as "Captain Bob."

After the surrender of the Confederacy in 1865, he returned to Memphis to resume his business career. At the age of 36 in 1873, when he became the first cashier of the Bank of Commerce, he was probably the youngest of the group of founders. He served as cashier of the bank through the first six years of its history. Although he left active service in the management of the bank in 1879, he continued his interest in banking and business throughout the remainder of his long life. For many years he served as an officer of J. T. Fargason & Company, wholesale grocers.

Robert Parker loved his city and maintained a strong interest in the activity of its downtown business district until his death. At the age of 92 he still maintained an office in the Porter Building, Memphis' first skyscraper which he saw during its construction in 1895. From his office he was able to watch the changing drama of Court Square which he considered the most historic site in the city. It was there he had first seen the flag of the Confederacy, under which he marched away to war, unfurled. It was in Court Square that he saw the young men of the city gather again to leave for the Spanish American War, and there also he saw young soldiers assemble once more to leave for service in World War I.

Although later in life he moved far eastward, to 1742 Central Avenue, he still made his daily journey to his office overlooking Court Square. Obviously possessed of a strong constitution, he had survived epidemics of smallpox, cholera and yellow fever — as well as the exposure, privations, marches, and battles of the Civil War. He continued to be interested in current affairs, business, and the history of his city until his death.

Robert A. Parker, Jr. died from influenza on December 29, 1928. At that time the Bank of Commerce and Trust Company, which he had helped establish more than half a century earlier, occupied a modern office building on Main Street just south of Madison Avenue. It was built on the land where his mother had planted her garden and grown cabbages and beans in 1841 when Main Street was a dirt road and the family's first cottage had stood behind its white-washed picket fence at Madison and Main. The *Memphis Press-Scimitar* described him as "the dean of Memphis bankers and one of the city's outstanding citizens and most lovable characters."

Perhaps the best known, and very likely the eldest, of the founders of the Bank of Commerce was Professor Eugene Magevney. Seventy-five years old in 1873, he had been born in 1798 in County Fermanagh, Ireland. After studying to become a Catholic priest, he decided to serve as a teacher instead. Although he first taught school in Ireland, he left his home as one of the early Irish immigrants to the United States. He taught school in Lebanon County, Pennsylvania, became an American citizen there, and then moved to Tennessee. In 1833, he arrived in Memphis at the age of 35. At that time the population of the city was less than

1,000, mainly living near the Mississippi River north of Court Square.

His first job was as the city's school teacher in a log structure the settlers had built in the forest that filled Court Square. This wooded area was outside the occupied portion of Memphis, but the residents had constructed a public building there because they feared that if they did not make some use of the square the real estate developers who had designated it for civic use when they laid out the city might reclaim it. The city had been developed by James Winchester, John Overton, and Andrew Jackson, whose interest was transferred to John C. McLemore.

Magevney taught school for seven years. But the year 1840 was an eventful one for him, for at that time he married and changed his profession. His marriage was to Mary Smyth, one of the pupils he had taught in Ireland. He finally sent for her to come to Memphis. They were married in the parlor of the home he had prepared for her on Adams Avenue. He had become a respected leader in the Catholic community of the city, and what historian Paul R. Coppock has described as the first Catholic mass in Memphis was celebrated in his home the year before the wedding.

Even before 1840, Eugene Magevney had begun to become involved in a new profession. There was no public money available for education, and school teachers were paid by the parents of the pupils they taught. Some of the upper-class families whose children he taught had more land than money. He began to receive part of his payments in parcels of land around the edge of the small city. After selling some tracts, he began to buy other properties. Some of these, including one on the south side of Union Avenue, became extremely valuable. He had the foresight to realize that this small, muddy town on the bank of the Mississippi River was destined to enter a period of phenomenal growth.

His vision was remarkable, and his actions based on it were uniformly profitable. Within two decades, according to the United States census, Memphis had

In the late 1800s, cotton was indeed king, and most of the fortunes made were based on its production and sale. Pictured here, the Mississippi riverboat Lady Lee *is docked at Memphis laden with bales of cotton, circa 1880.*

become the largest city in Tennessee and the sixth largest in the entire South. He gave up teaching permanently to devote all of his time to a new career as a real estate investor. By purchasing land just outside of the settled areas and selling it at appreciated value as the city continued to grow, he accumulated a fortune ultimately worth several million dollars. He was able to retain control of his properties through the troubled times of war, military occupation, and Reconstruction. Although advanced in years and near the end of his life in April 1873, he brought strength to the leadership of the bank by his widespread respect, his business experience, and his unshakable belief in the continued growth of his city.

J. T. Fargason brought to the Board of Directors a thorough background and unsurpassed record of success in the cotton business, the most important economic activity in the development of Memphis during the 19th century. Born on his family's cotton plantation in Chambers County, Alabama, he was a descendant of several generations of planters who had operated large landholdings in Georgia and Alabama. He started his adult life as a cotton planter himself, but left Alabama when the economy there was disrupted by the Civil War.

Arriving in Memphis during 1863, he obviously brought some of his financial resources and all of his ambition and business sense with him. Although he was only 28 years old at the time, and he found Memphis under federal military occupation, he allowed neither his youth nor the Union army to interfere with the beginning of his rapid rise to prominence. He achieved success both as a planter and as an urban businessman who provided the services needed by other planters in the area. Beginning to acquire fertile agricultural land, which was readily available during the era, he increased his holdings until he was the owner of several large cotton plantations in the Mid-South area of Tennessee, Mississippi, and Arkansas. One of these, a 5,200-acre plantation at Clover Hill, Mississippi, was still operated by one of his descendants almost a century after his arrival in Memphis.

Cotton was indeed king when the tri-state area was being settled and developed, and most of the fortunes made were based on its production and sale. J. T. Fargason, however, had the sharpness of judgment to see that even more profit could be made by those who supplied and financed the planters and stored, shipped, and speculated in the commodity.

Accordingly, young Fargason decided to become a cotton factor as well as a planter. Without waiting for the Union occupation to end, he succeeded in establishing a cotton firm under the name of Fargason and Clay. During the next decade the firm's name was changed to J. T. Fargason and Company. Located on Front Street, this cotton factor and wholesale grocery business often had annual sales of about $1.2 million and handled as many as 30,000 bales of cotton per season. Every one of these bales produced a profit for the firm.

As will be noted in subsequent chapters, Fargason continued to provide principal leadership to the Bank of Commerce for more than the first third of a century of its existence — until his death in 1909. It is a reasonable assumption that his influence and business contacts played a part in making the bank the major source of financial support for the cotton industry in the Mid-South.

Considerably less information is available about the other business and civic leaders who made up the first Board of Directors of the Bank of Commerce. Nathan Adams had achieved success and wealth as an insurance executive in the city before the founding of the bank in 1873. There was a close relationship between the insurance and banking businesses in Memphis at this time. Before a strong and safely managed banking system was developed, many investors considered it more prudent to place their money with insurance companies. Actually, both banks and insurance companies had experienced a high rate of failure in the South prior to the 1870s. Much of the capital previously invested with insurance companies would become available for deposit in banks when the public could be convinced that they were safe, solvent, and capably managed. It is a fair conclusion that the insurance experience of Nathan Adams was an asset to the bank.

Oliver Hazard Perry Piper was a veteran of the Confederacy who had become successful as a construction contractor. During the remainder of the 19th century, Memphis was to more than double in population, expand its settled area, and experience a substantial increase in new construction. The appearance of electrical power, the invention of the elevator, and the development of new building materials and techniques during this era gave rise to a renaissance of urban construction. Except for interruptions during times of depression, building activity was constant in Memphis, both in areas where the city was expanding outward and downtown where the skyline began to assume a new configuration as older structures were replaced by larger and taller ones. Contacts with this industry were of obvious importance to the bank.

The two remaining members of the Board of Directors made their own contributions to the institution. Thomas H. Allen, a respected and experienced cotton merchant, added his familiarity with the major economic activity of the region to that of J. T. Fargason. In fact, the boards of directors of lending institutions in the Mid-South were generally dominated by cotton men. Businessmen involved in newly developing entrepreneurial activities, such as the hardwood lumber industry, often complained that they could not borrow sufficient investment capital because so much of the money available for loans was absorbed by cotton plantations and firms.

Howell E. Jackson was an experienced attorney well known in the legal and business circles of the city. If there were ever a time when a major financial institution did not need capable legal counsel at the managerial level, that time had passed forever by the 1870s. Leading attorneys have served as members of banking boards to the present.

Together, these nine Memphians provided the resources and collective judgment necessary to found a successful new financial institution.

While the wisdom and experience of the founders were the most important assets of the newly established Bank of Commerce, its most important symbol to the general population the founders hoped to attract as customers was the building in which it was located. Because the success of financial institutions depends on the trust and respect of the individuals they serve, bankers have usually been aware of the importance of the appearance of their buildings. Even today, in the latter part of the 20th century, much of the major building construction in the business areas of Southern cities has been done by large banks, and in smaller towns throughout the region the most impressive and architecturally advanced structures are generally those of the local banks.

Completely familiar with their city, the founders of the Bank of Commerce surveyed Memphis for the best possible site for their new enterprise. They found it at

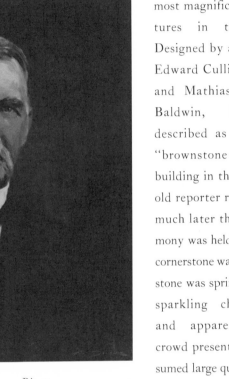

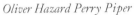

Oliver Hazard Perry Piper .

12 Madison Street. (All of the Memphis street addresses were renumbered early in the 20th century, and many of the east-west streets were renamed as avenues.) Almost new at that date, it had been built just three years earlier by the Merchants Insurance Company. The firm had spared no cost in constructing it, and it was considered one of the most magnificent structures in the city. Designed by architects Edward Culliatt Jones and Mathias Harvey Baldwin, it was described as the first "brownstone front" building in the city. An old reporter recollected much later that a ceremony was held when the cornerstone was laid. The stone was sprinkled with sparkling champagne and apparently the crowd present also consumed large quantities of the beverage.

No more respectable location could have been found. The financial heart of Memphis, which had become known as "bankers' row," was located along both sides of Madison Street between Main Street on the east and Front Street on the west. The new Bank of Commerce building was located on the north side of Madison at the northwest corner of an alley that intersected this block at the halfway point. Other financial businesses lined both sides of Madison.

These surroundings gave a sense of respectability and prosperity. Furthermore, the influence of the financial center of Memphis extended over a wide geographical area. In this era when the United States was beginning a period of great urban growth, the Bluff

City had no nearby rivals. To the north, the nearest city of comparable or greater size was St. Louis. Southward, the nearest competitor was New Orleans. None of the cities to the southwest had begun to boom, and to the east, along the line of the old Memphis and Charleston Railroad, there were no larger cities nearer than the Atlantic coast. Atlanta, Nashville, and Birmingham were all smaller than Memphis. Thus bankers in this Mid-South center had opportunities in their own urban area and also in a broad expanse of the richest cotton producing land in the nation.

As a result of the good judgment of its founders in selecting the building at 12 Madison Street, the Bank of Commerce had the advantage of the most impressive site in the financial district of bankers' row. A sketch published in a *Harper's Weekly* feature entitled "Views in Memphis, Tenn." shows the structure at 12 Madison towering above its neighboring buildings on both sides of the street. This avenue, wide for a Southern city of the time, seems to have been paved with cobblestones. Although this surface provided a rough ride in wheeled vehicles, it was the best material available. Most of the city streets were still of dirt and mud, but part of the downtown area had been furnished with Nicolson pavement, wood blocks fitted together to form a hard surface, that was

Created in 1887, this engraving depicts Madison Street, looking toward Front Street, known as "bankers' row." The Bank of Commerce's tower (at right) may have been added to extend the height of the building above that of other banks in the area.

completely unsatisfactory. The wood tended to rot quickly in wet soil, to break under heavy usage, and to become saturated with animal excrement from the thousands of horses and mules that drew wagons and carriages along the street.

The view to the west along Madison Street from the bank was unimpeded across Front Street, the promenade, the smoke-stacks of steamboats at the landing, and the Mississippi River into Arkansas. A lithograph, dated 1870, now in the Library of Congress, shows no buildings along the west side of Front Street north of Union Avenue. The massive United States Customs House, Courthouse, and Post Office at this site was not constructed until 1876, although the first appropriation for it was approved almost two months before the bank opened. A portion of this building, best known in Memphis as the Customs House, still exists today as part of the downtown post office.

The building in which the Bank of Commerce opened was both its operational headquarters and its symbol of integrity and prosperity. Although the edifice might seem strange today, in that Victorian era when architectural elaborateness was admired, it was considered "the handsomest building" in town. Eugene J. Johnson and Robert D. Russell, in their book, *Memphis An Architectural Guide*, wrote as follows of the bank and its street: "...lined with bank buildings that competed eagerly with each other in architectural pretension. Perhaps most remarkable of them was the Bank of Commerce Building."

What modern authors, writing about the creative works of previous ages, sometimes misunderstand is that structures which may seem pretentious today did not seem ostentatious at all when they were built. Memphians of the 1870s seemingly considered the building to be the epitome of style. It is difficult, however, to describe the style of the building, mainly because of its complexity. Contemporary sketches give the appearance that the architects had deliberately made an effort to design a single structure containing as many different elements of style as possible.

It was constructed with three main floors, each with a much higher than usual ceiling. The first floor was entered by two sets of steps, one at each side of the entrance on Madison Street. Three pointed arches flanked by eight engaged columns faced the street. Large block letters, "Bank of Commerce," were incised across the entire stone wall of the front above the arches. The second story was completely different in style. Three arches of a different style were set between four engaged columns with corbels placed above them. The third main floor was even more elaborate, including nine columns and a system of arches within other arches. Above these were additional columns and more decorative detail in the stone facade. Two gabled towers, one on each side, rose even higher. Between them, another tower, reminiscent of New England style, extended even higher. This last element may have been added to extend the height of the building above that of the others in the area. Its general appearance was gothic, but the variety of architectural styles in the different stories makes a single description difficult.

Nonetheless, it was a practical as well as imposing site. The entrances were well designed for public use and the building obviously contained a large amount of floor space. The height was about as great as was reasonable for any firm doing business with the public before the introduction of elevators. It was not until after the bank had opened that the management of the Peabody Hotel proudly announced the installation of an early model of the hydraulic elevator.

Heat was provided by pot-bellied iron stoves which were relatively new to use in the city. Coal for these stoves was probably stored in a part of the basement. Most residents of the area were still using wood for fuel. Wood could be bought cheaply from local suppliers, but coal was more expensive since it had to be shipped from the north by steamboat. The very high ceilings on all the floors helped the bank employees keep cool during the hot summers.

The water supply was drawn from a basement cistern which was kept filled by rainwater collected through a system of drains from the roof. Though this water was not clean by current standards, it was better than most available. Cisterns of private homes were generally contaminated by the drainage of sewage in the ground since Memphis had no sewer system. The city council in 1873 chartered a private waterworks company that opened service by providing water to 436 customers, but since their water was pumped from the polluted Wolf River, it is doubtful that they were safer than other residents.

Thus the Bank of Commerce opened at a prime location in a structure that was well adapted for its needs as well as an admired architectural landmark of the city. In this respect, the men who were the founders of the bank deserve appropriate credit. They established a precedent, which has been followed by subsequent officers and directors, of maintaining structures that represent the qualities of what a successful bank ought to be to the people of their city. Through all of its history, the Bank of Commerce has been responsible for some of the most respected and admired architecture in Memphis.

Early businessmen found that profit could be made in supplying, financing, storing, and shipping cotton. Pictured here, the Mississippi riverboat Sadie Lee *awaits departure from the Memphis riverfront with a load of the commodity.*

CHAPTER TWO

THE DEVELOPMENT OF MEMPHIS TO APRIL 1873

Memphis, founded as a real estate development in 1819, was started in an excellent location, but at an unfortunate time. During this year, the first major depression in the American business cycle began and this event caused settlement of the new city to be slow. According to the United States census of 1820, the entire population of Memphis included only 53 people. During the 1820s, the population increased gradually and some small businesses were established. By the close of the decade, the region of the Mid-South was entering a period of prosperity. A major handicap to business development, though, was the lack of capital. Only a limited amount of currency circulated in the national economy, and very little of it made its way as far westward as the new settlement on the Mississippi River.

There was no banking institution in Memphis during this decade. Residents dealt with this problem to a degree by an extensive system of barter in which they exchanged goods and services with one another. The money used in the city was paper notes issued by Tennessee, North Carolina, South Carolina, and Georgia. This was depreciated currency in relation to United States coinage. Even when these notes were valid, and counterfeiting was not uncommon, they were usually accepted only at a discount at locations distant from the place where they were issued. When Memphis residents had to buy goods from eastern merchants, their money was accepted at a discount of 25 percent or more.

Without a local bank available, Memphians continued to experience great inconvenience from the perpetual lack of capital. This situation was described by early Memphis historian J. P. Young who said, "...almost everybody in Memphis was in debt and the rule was credit with long time, because money was loaned at such exorbitant rates, sometimes as high as 6 percent a month." The first Memphis merchants, such as Marcus Winchester and Isaac Rawlings, apparently alleviated this problem to an extent by extending credit to local customers.

The growth of Memphis had been so slow during the first decade of its history that most residents probably did not realize the great significance to them of the events that had taken place outside of their city. By the close of the decade, the foundations of the future growth and prosperity had already been laid, even though they did not realize it at the time. There had been two changes of paramount importance. One had taken place on the rivers and the other had occurred on the land. They were the construction of steamboats and the establishment of plantations.

The Mississippi River, flowing by the western boundary of Memphis, was the greatest natural commercial artery in the United States. As settlers flooded westward during the period between the American Revolution and the 1820s, the volume of merchandise carried on its waters increased greatly, but there was one major limitation to this trade. Almost all freight could be moved in only one direction — downstream. The greatest event in the history of river commerce in the United States was the invention of the steamboat.

The first of these had traveled past the Chickasaw Bluffs during its voyage from Pittsburgh to New Orleans in 1811, but improvements in design and engines had to be made before they could be used effectively for travel up the river. When Memphis was founded in 1819, they were just beginning to be used successfully. A series of technical improvements took place during the 1820s, and the number of these vessels on the rivers increased.

The establishment of cotton plantations was as important to Memphis as the invention of steamboats. The city had the good fortune to be founded in one of the most fertile agricultural areas of the nation, but because all of West Tennessee was opened to settlement at the same time, the plantations had not been created when Memphis was founded. By 1825, however, planters had started sending their cotton to Memphis. The first bales were carried by wagons over primitive roads and by boats along wilderness rivers and creeks filled with snags and drifts. The first cotton sales in the city amounted to only a few hundred bales per year, but the volume was due to increase.

There was a dynamic energy in the early cotton business in the Mid-South. It would succeed because these planters were determined to make it successful, whatever obstacles they might encounter. This energy and ambition was communicated to the businessmen of Memphis who saw the opportunities in an interrelated economy in which their city could prosper as its hinterland did. It was this symbiotic relationship of mutual benefit that directed Memphis during the decade of the 1830s to its beginning as a cotton port, a transportation center, and a provider of banking services.

When the United States census was taken in 1830, the population of the city had increased to 663, and it would almost triple within the next decade. It was this growth of population and an even greater growth of business that made the establishment of a banking system imperative. The first bank that was organized received its charter from the Tennessee General Assembly on December 4, 1833. It was badly needed.

The amount of capital available was far from adequate for the needs of a city that was beginning to grow. The amount of the United States coinage in circulation had increased, but most local transactions still had to rely on the discounted paper notes of various states. To make change, these bills were cut into four equal pieces for quarters. Sometimes these quarters were again cut in half to make "bits" with a value of twelve and a half cents each.

The expanding cotton business was handled almost entirely on credit. The planters, despite their increasing production and profits, generally had almost no cash. Their operations, and often their lavish styles of living, were expanding too rapidly for them to save any money. They usually spent all the money they could get in this era of growth, and secured the maximum amount of credit available in the often justified expectation of increasing profits in the future. A new group of urban businessmen began to operate during this decade, with such success that they became the financial leaders of Memphis during much of the century. They were the cotton factors, or commission merchants, whose business was to supply on credit all the needs of the self-contained economic empires of the Mid-South cotton plantations. Early every year they began to provide the planters of the area with the seed, clothing, food, tools, agricultural machinery, medicine, furnishings, and other items needed to support their large operations through the season. Every fall, when the white gold of the cotton crops was ready for market, these factors, who held first lien on the crops, handled the sales. At this time, they collected payment for the goods they had provided, and profited further by charging a commission for handling every bale of cotton sold.

It was this economic system that required the support of organized financial institutions. The pioneer bank of the city, and thus the predecessor of all subsequent banking businesses, was the Farmers and Merchants Bank of Memphis, chartered in 1833. The list of presidents of the bank includes: N. Anderson, Robert Lawrence, P. W. Lucas, Seth

Wheatley, and Jephtha Fowlkes. The members of the board of directors in later years continued to represent the financial aristocracy of the city. Paul Garland wrote: "The people involved in creating this bank were the actual first citizens of Memphis, as many as four of the first Mayors of Memphis were officers and stockholders."

The bank maintained profitable operations for 20 years, enthusiastically supported by the residents who had been in such need of its services. This pioneer bank sought, as such institutions must, the patronage of businesses and wealthy individuals. It also, however, welcomed the accounts of ordinary citizens in large numbers. A fact little known today is that part of the business of the bank was done with slaves. Some urban slaves in that era had more freedom than is generally realized, and in some cases were encouraged by their owners to save their money. J. P. Young wrote, "Marcus B. Winchester opened a regular account with all of his slaves, charging them with their purchase money, food, clothing, etc., and crediting them with all of their labor, with the view to their buying their freedom." More slaves than is generally recognized were able to secure their freedom. By 1860, during the last decade of slavery, there were about 7,300 free persons of African-American descent in Tennessee, the greatest numbers of them residing in Nashville, Memphis, and Knoxville. All customers, regardless of color, were apparently accepted as depositors at this bank.

Another financial institution was organized in the city in 1835, the Memphis Banking Company. The principals in its formation were McKee, Young and Company; Fowlkes and Pugh; Dixon, Strong and Company; and T. G. Johnson. Information about its capitalization and operations is unavailable and very few notes seem to have been issued. It may have functioned mainly as a private bank for a limited number of customers.

The decade of the 1830s, although mainly known for its prosperity, ended in hard times and disaster for many people. Having recovered from the depression of the 1820s, the region entered a period of economic boom characterized by unrestrained speculation, unstable currency, over-extended credit, and inadequate capital. The national financial panic of 1837 and the following depression brought years of distress.

The decade of the 1840s began with the population of the city at 1,799, and the economic foundation of the Mid-South area still basically sound. Memphis' population, and thus the volume of its business activity, was just entering an era of rapid growth, and the advantage of its incomparable location on a bluff of the greatest river in the continent at the center of a great agricultural region was sufficient to prevail over the effects of the national depression. During this decade, Memphis became one of the leading cities in the South.

The motive force that drove this urban growth was the cotton industry. Prices continued to be favorable for the staple. It became money as soon as it could be grown and sent to market in Memphis. New acreage was cleared and the profits increased. Columned mansions, some of which still stand, began to appear on the larger plantations. Planters and farmers with money provided a growing market for retail goods from the city. Cotton brought wealth to the rural Mid-South, but it made the urban factors and other middlemen even richer. The economic growth of the city was based directly on the flow of cotton. In 1840, 35,000 bales were sold in Memphis. Through the decade, this total increased steadily to an annual sale of 163,000 bales — a growth of more than 365 percent. During this period the value of cotton sold in the city annually rose from $1.4 million to $6.5 million.

Memphis' success as a cotton market was based on transportation of the product into and out of the city. The unanticipated growth of this industry made improvements in commercial travel by land and water a prime necessity. Business and financial leaders carried on a crusade through the decade to make Memphis a transportation center of the South.

River transportation was most important at the beginning. By 1840, most of the Mississippi River had

Steamboats carried cotton out of Memphis, but land transportation was needed to bring it into the city. Road building was especially difficult. A solution to the road problem appeared with the development of railroads.

been cleared of snags and an average of more than two steamboats were stopping at the city each day. There were 450 of these in operation on the river in 1843. Their numbers continued to increase every year. By the close of the decade, packet boats kept regular schedules from Memphis to Cincinnati, Louisville, and New Orleans.

Steamboats carried cotton out of Memphis, but land transportation was needed to bring it into the city. Road building was especially difficult. The loose, fertile soil that made agriculture so successful was not suitable for roads during much of the year, and no effective form of paving was available. A solution to the road problem appeared with the development of railroads. The Memphis and LaGrange Railroad had

been chartered in 1835, but construction eastward was slow. In 1840, John C. McLemore assumed its leadership. Within two years a train was operating through the rural area to Buntyn with construction under way as far as White Station. Financial problems delayed further construction until later, but the demand for railroad building continued. Another railroad, the Memphis and Ohio, was chartered in 1842 to build a line northward, but lack of capital also delayed its construction until the next decade.

A prosperous business community dominated the new city. According to author Gerald Capers, there were two flour mills and two machine works in operation. The large Curtis and Knapp Foundry was building steamboats. M. E. Cochran and Company operated a planing mill and a door, sash, blind, and box factory. The Bolen and Wilson Ice Company sold ice from Illinois to local residents. In addition to numerous retail outlets, there was a thriving regional distribution community in the city. Some of the wholesale food, dry goods, hardware, and clothing firms in operation during the decade were B. Lowenstein and Brothers; J. F. Frank and Company; Bransford, Goodbar and Company; Orgill Brothers; Shepard and Moore; C. W. Goyer and Company; and S. Mansfield and Company.

Memphis banking had also begun to grow. The Farmers and Merchants Bank, which had temporarily suspended operations because of a run by its depositors, had reopened for business. Two new banks, both branches of successful Nashville institutions, had been established. The Memphis branch of the Union Bank of Tennessee was the first of these. It was chartered in 1839, and established in 1841 with a capital of $150,000. By 1850, it had moved to an address on Madison Street. Its parent bank in Nashville was an unusually strong one for a Southern city, having a capitalization of $3 million. One half of its stock was owned by a group of Philadelphia capitalists and one sixth was owned by the state of Tennessee.

Its Memphis branch operated profitably until after the outbreak of the Civil War. The successive record of presidents of this bank includes John Pope, A. R. Herron, and Samuel Mosby, who served until 1862. There is, however, an unexplained question about this bank. One source mentions that the president in 1865 was Edgar McDavitt, who later appears as the first president of the Bank of Commerce. This report may be an error, because the bank closed in Memphis in June 1862, when its assets were moved away to the south for safety inside Confederate lines.

The second of the banks to be established in the city in the decade was the Memphis branch of the Planters Bank of Tennessee. It was established in 1842, at Main and Washington streets with a capital of $150,000. Its parent bank had been founded nine years earlier in Nashville with a capital of $2 million. Like

the Union Bank, it operated successfully until more than a year after the beginning of the Civil War. Its assets were removed and taken south into Confederate territory in May 1862, the month before the fall of Memphis. Its presidents were John W. Goff, Jacob N. Moon, James Elder, and Edgar McDavitt, who served from 1858 until 1865, although during the last three of these years he apparently remained in Memphis while the assets were elsewhere. It is evident that he brought considerable successful banking experience with him when he later assumed the presidency of the Bank of Commerce.

The decade of the 1850s was a time of great municipal growth for Memphis. The population grew more than 150 percent, from 8,841 to 22,623, a smaller percentage than in the 1840s, but greater than in any decade since. It was a time of dynamic progress in business and transportation. The Mississippi River continued to carry most of the city's passengers and freight. Steamboats became larger and more elegant and each year their number increased. By 1860, packet boats were in general use, and an estimated 30 steamboats were owned in or operated from Memphis.

One of the most important events in the history of Memphis took place in May 1857. It was the arrival of a special train that had traveled over a newly completed railroad from Charleston, South Carolina. This highly publicized occasion was marked by the largest celebration that had been held in the Mississippi River city, and that was probably not equalled until the dedication of the structure designated the Great American Pyramid in the 1990s. The Memphis and Charleston Railroad was formed by a connection of the Memphis and LaGrange Railroad which had been extended eastward to meet a line built from Charleston. This new line was the only one in the South connecting the Atlantic coast with the Mississippi River. It opened an entire new area to commerce with Memphis.

Business growth in the city continued through the 1850s. A report by the chamber of commerce at the end of the decade listed annual business receipts in the city at more than $52 million. The leading products were cotton, dry goods, hardware, bacon, and flour, although 75 other products also were sold in the city.

Although cotton had accounted for most of the business expansion during the 1840s, it was banking that demonstrated the greatest growth during the 1850s. Paul R. Coppock, a 20th century Memphis historian, has assembled extensive information about these financial institutions from the *Bankers Register* for 1860. The three largest were branches of Nashville banks, that city having the advantage of an early start toward becoming a financial center before Memphis was founded.

The largest capital was listed for the Memphis branch of the Bank of Tennessee, with James Lenow as president and N. L. Lawrence as cashier. It had a $300,000 capital, although as was the case with all local branches, the parent bank listed a much greater amount. The Memphis branch of the Union Bank of Tennessee, with Samuel Mosby as president and Frederick W. Smith as cashier, listed a capital of $150,000. The Memphis branch of the Planters Bank of Tennessee had Edgar McDavitt (later the first president of the Bank of Commerce) as president and James Penn as cashier. It had a listed capital of $150,000.

There were five locally owned banks in Memphis at this time. The largest of these was the River Bank of Tennessee. Capitalized at $100,000, it listed D. N. Kennedy as president and W. S. McClure as the cashier. The Commercial Bank, with a capital of $50,000, was served by W. M. Fotwell as president and J. W. Page as the cashier. The Bank of Memphis, with M. J. Wicks as president and W. C. McClure as cashier, had capital of $50,000. The Bank of West Tennessee, capitalized at the same amount, listed J. M. Wiliamson as president and J. A. Sannoner as cashier. The other locally owned institution, the Southern Bank, served by W. J. Davie as president and W. Moore as cashier, did not have a listed capital, but it was probably not large.

A review of the locations of these banks in the 1860 city directory reveals that the financial district, or "bankers' row," was beginning to develop on Madison Street between Main and Front. The *Bankers Register* also listed five private banks and bankers, some of them associated with insurance companies in the city. No information was listed about their assets, but it seems that their service was mainly to a limited number of selected clients. This rapidly developed collection of Memphis banks had little competition in providing service throughout a wide geographical area. There were only two additional banks in all of the remainder of West Tennessee, both branches of the Bank of Tennessee. One was located at Trenton and the other at Somerville.

These Memphis banks provided services to their city and the region in which it was located at the beginning of the 1860s. The Bluff City had passed Nashville to become the largest in the state. It continued to gain population throughout the decade, from 22,263 to 40,246, but much of this increase was a result of wartime growth and the migration of large numbers of former slaves from the countryside. The greatest age in the expansion of Memphis banking was over. Dramatic and memorable events took place during the decade. They were mainly military, social, and political in nature. The two major influences on the city during the 1860s were the Civil War and Reconstruction, both highly disruptive to business and finance.

The fate of Memphis banking during the decade reveals some of the extent of the financial troubles. The Bank of West Tennessee had to suspend operations during the federal occupation. The owners tried to resume operations after the war, but it soon went into receivership. The Commercial Bank of Tennessee began to fail within a year after the capture of the city, and its affairs were all closed over a period of several years by its appointed receiver, James A. Omberg. His success in this duty helped prepare him for his later position as cashier of the Bank of Commerce. Another financial enterprise, the Gayoso Savings Institution, which did some general banking, also declined during the decade and went into receivership in 1869. The Memphis Life and General Insurance Company, which did some banking business, was forced to close during the war. It attempted to resume operations at the close of the war, but survived only a few years. As the capture of the city became imminent, the owners of the Memphis branch of the Planters Bank of Tennessee removed its assets to the south. They were eventually taken to the parent bank in Nashville. The Memphis branch of the Union Bank of Tennessee also had its assets removed so that they would not fall into federal hands. The bank was formally closed after the end of the war. The River Bank, as a result of wartime disruption of its operations, was forced into liquidation before the city fell to Union military forces. Since Memphis was captured early in the war, all its financial business after June 1862 was transacted in United States currency, which of course retained its value after the war.

Moreover, the city still had its great advantage of location on the Mississippi River and in the center of the rich agricultural area of the Mid-South. The land was not damaged by the war, and the network of roads and railroads built during antebellum times was still in existence. Although the process required several years, the production of cotton recovered after the war. A system of sharecropping soon took the place of slavery as a source of labor to produce cotton. In this manner, the decade of the Civil War and Reconstruction came to a close. The decade of the 1870s, in which visionary survivors of the wartime experience met to form the Bank of Commerce, was to be an era of rebuilding.

CHARTER AND BY-LAWS

OF THE

BANK OF COMMERCE

NO. 12 MADISON STREET,

MEMPHIS, TENNESSEE.

ADOPTED JULY 2, 1889.

1889
TRACY PRINTING CO., MEMPHIS.

All officers of the Bank of Commerce were required to take an oath not to willfully or knowingly violate any direction or provision of the bank's charter and bylaws.

CHAPTER THREE

AN AUSPICIOUS BEGINNING:
SUCCESS THROUGH TROUBLED TIMES

Considering the recurrent upward and downward fluctuations of the national economy throughout the history of American banking, it is important that a new financial institution should start with as great a position of strength as possible. It is helpful also if the founders of a bank have either the good fortune or the exceptional foresight to start their enterprise in a favorable curve of the business cycle. Although there were both local and national difficulties ahead that probably no business leaders could foresee, on the basis of information available at the time, the year of the founding of the Bank of Commerce seemed to be a propitious time.

Thus the decision was made to begin the operations of the bank in 1873. The historical evidence that the Bank of Commerce opened its doors for business in April of this year is unquestionably clear. There is, however, an unexplained anomaly about the bank's beginning. A state court decision during the 1890s, about the tax obligations of the Bank of Commerce, referred to its charter which was issued "before the Civil War." Since no copy of the documents reviewed by the court in making this decision have been found, the enigma of how a bank founded eight years after the Civil War could operate under the terms of a charter issued before the war has created a mystery.

Attempts to solve this puzzle have led in several different directions, but all clues have led toward the establishment of some other financial institution during antebellum times in another Tennessee city. There still exists at present, in 1993, a legend passed down orally to senior officers of National Bank of Commerce of some previous connection with a bank in Chattanooga. A reasonable hypothesis was that the charter of an earlier institution in Chattanooga had been acquired by the founders of the Bank of Commerce.

One speculation about this early banking connection, which has been proven to be incorrect, was that

the founders of the Bank of Commerce might in some way have acquired the charter of an earlier institution, the Bank of Memphis, which was chartered on September 1, 1853. This organization operated, apparently at a profit, for seven years with R. C. Brinkley, John Overton, and W. J. Wicks serving successively as president. Despite this successful record, it surrendered its charter in 1860. According to Chapter 49 of the Private Acts of the General Assembly of the State of Tennessee, 1859-1860, an act was passed to withdraw the Bank of Memphis and establish in lieu thereof a branch of the Bank of Chattanooga at Memphis. The stock in both institutions was held by the same stockholders, and it was at their request that the legislature passed this act. Their reason for requesting this change was not reported, and it may have been simply to secure unified management of their two enterprises. In less than a year afterward, the breakup of the Union and the secession of the Confederate states began. This proposed new branch bank apparently never had an opportunity to begin operations. Although there were business and family connections between the men who were active in the early Bank of Memphis and the later Bank of Commerce, it is now clear that there was no line of succession between the two institutions.

The actual record of the institutions that were the predecessors of the Bank of Commerce is different, although it is quite complicated and does include a Chattanooga connection. So far as the record reveals, the account began on February 29, 1856, although considerable planning and prearrangement had obviously been done previously. On that date the Tennessee General Assembly passed two acts important in the financial history of the state. The legislature passed these acts, as has often been its custom, at the behest of wealthy investors. And it was no mere coincidence that both were passed on the same day.

They first authorized Memphis businessmen Jesse E. Maxwell, A. D. Witherspoon, A. J. White, William E. Milton, and Gabriel Smither to create "a body politic and corporate, by the name and style of the Gayoso Savings Institution." It provided that the capital stock of the company would be divided into shares of $50 each, and when 200 of these shares were subscribed, the stockholders could elect officers and open for business. The location of the institution was not stipulated in the act, but the use of the name Gayoso, a former Spanish governor of Louisiana whose name had been given to various sites in Memphis, indicated that the Bluff City was the intended location of the company.

In addition to the usual details of corporate organization and duties, the act provided that the Gayoso Savings Institution would "pay to the State an annual tax of one-half of one per cent on each share of capital stock, which shall be in lieu of all other taxes." The act further provided: "That said institution may discount notes, buy and sell stock, deal in exchange, and gold and silver bullion; may purchase and hold a lot of ground for the use of the institution, as a place of business, and at pleasure sell or exchange the same; and may hold such real or personal property and estate as may be conveyed to it to secure debts due the institution; and may sell and convey the same; it may receive on deposit any and all sums, not less than one dollar per week, offered as stock deposits...it may receive other general or special deposits, and allow such interest

thereon as may be agreed upon, not exceeding that allowed by law; and twice per year declare and pay to stockholders a dividend of interest."

Although the word "bank" was not included in the act, the "savings institution" it created was empowered to conduct a banking business. It is listed under Memphis banks in Paul E. Garland's *The History of Early Tennessee Banks and Their Issues*. According to Garland's book, it was organized by December 1856, with a paid-up capital of $50,000, which was subsequently increased to $100,000. It was located at 19 Madison Street. This was across the street and a short distance east of 12 Madison. Thus it was located within a stone's throw of the site of its future successor, the Bank of Commerce. The Gayoso Savings Institution paid 6 percent on deposits during its first year. The officers when it opened were A. M. Foute, president; E. M. Avery, cashier; J. M. White, C. J. Selden, and John Winbish, directors. Even though this institution operated under the direction of its local officers in Memphis, its ownership was headquartered in Chattanooga.

The second act passed by the Tennessee General Assembly, by evident coordination and prearrangement of the Chattanooga investors, was "An Act to Incorporate the Gayoso Savings Institution and the Chattanooga Savings Institution." It provided: "That Benjamin Chandler, Samuel R. McCamy, James Whiteside, John L. M. French, Edwin Marsh and James C. Warner, their associates and successors, be, and they are hereby created a body politic and corporate, by the name and style of the Chattanooga Savings Institution, and by that name shall have succession, sue and be sued, plead and be impleaded; and they are hereby invested with all the powers, privileges, rights and immunities, and subjected to the same liabilities and restrictions that are given and imposed in the foregoing sections upon the Gayoso Savings Institution. The Corporation chartered by this section shall be located in the City of Chattanooga."

Despite this location of ownership and controlling

interest in Chattanooga, it seems that the Memphis institution continued to operate and apparently did so under the Gayoso name. In fact, it may be that the institution in Memphis operated with more success than the Chattanooga owners expected. Memphis' population and business prosperity had grown much greater than that of its East Tennessee neighbor. The next legislative action concerning these two institutions took place on November 15, 1859. Its record reads as follows: "An Act to Authorize the Chattanooga Savings Institution to Remove their Office to Memphis, Tennessee. Be it enacted by the General Assembly of the State of Tennessee, That the Chattanooga Savings Institution be, and they are hereby authorized to remove their office to Memphis, Tennessee."

It may be that this authorization was never acted upon. The timing of the move was seemingly left to the discretion of the stockholders. By the time this act was passed, the stresses which would divide the nation the next year had already become acute. In Tennessee, these issues involved increasing antipathy between the eastern and western parts of the state. Paul Garland's book reports that the Gayoso Savings Institution continued to be in business in Memphis throughout the years of the war. Moreover, it seems to have operated more successfully than financial institutions did in Chattanooga.

This estimate is supported by the next legislative action affecting these institutions. Passed on February 12, 1866, this act was worded as follows: "Be it enacted by the General Assembly of the State of Tennessee, That An Act to authorize the Chattanooga Savings Institution to remove their office to Memphis, Tennessee, passed November 15, 1859, be so amended as to change the name from the 'Chattanooga Savings Institution,' to 'The Savings Bank of Memphis,' and that this Act take effect from and after its passage."

The name change was put into effect, although the removal of the office to Memphis may not have been made, for there is no record of a bank by this new name actually doing business in the Bluff City. Meanwhile, the Gayoso Savings Institution, having survived the wartime years, began to experience trouble during the Reconstruction era. Garland stated that: "It became involved in difficulties which resulted in a run on it, and in February 1870, its doors were closed. This failure caused considerable loss and created intense excitement among depositors." This account of its closing is confusing, for it also stated, "Samuel Mosby was appointed receiver in 1869 and wound up the affairs of the institution." Whatever the sequence of events may have been, it is clear that it was no longer in business by the beginning of the 1870s.

The next episode in this complicated business epic took place on March 12, 1873. On this date, the Tennessee legislature passed the following act: "Be it enacted by the General Assembly of the State of Tennessee, That the Act of this General Assembly, passed February 12, 1866, be so amended as to change the name of 'Savings Bank of Memphis,' to the 'Bank of Commerce,' and that this act take effect from and after its passage, the public welfare requiring the same." The long saga of the development of this financial institution thus ended in 1873 with the founding of a new bank that would endure long past the lives of all people living at the time.

An interesting observation about the history of Memphis banks may be drawn from this story of succession. It can be maintained that the existence of the Bank of Commerce did indeed begin when it opened its doors at 12 Madison Street in 1873. If, however, it is considered that the history of the bank began when its charter did in 1856, as the subsequent court decision accepted, a case could be made that it is now, in 1993, the oldest bank in Memphis.

The Bank of Commerce began its existence with a highly organized and carefully detailed set of bylaws. A reading of the 37 sections of this document, which filled nine printed pages, gives a revealing view of the structure and operating procedures of the institution. It compels admiration by a modern reader of the experience and wisdom of the founders who drafted and adopted it.

Control of the bank was exercised by its stockholders who held a meeting annually on the second Tuesday of April to elect officers and directors for the forthcoming year. Procedures for conducting this election were specifically prescribed. The officers, at the beginning, were a president, cashier, teller, bookkeeper, and such other officers as might be required for the prompt and orderly transaction of its business. The cashier and the subordinate officers were to serve at the pleasure of the Board of Directors, and the cashier was given the duty, "carefully to observe the conduct of all persons employed under him, and to report to the Board such instances of neglect, absence, incapacity, or bad conduct in any of them, as shall come to his knowledge." The office of vice president did not exist at the beginning, but was added soon afterward.

The cashier served under a bond of $30,000, the teller $20,000, and each clerk $10,000. The bylaws provided that: "Every Clerk or person in the employ of the Bank shall give his attendance and labor in the same, as long as his services may be required by the regular business, or by the Cashier, the President or the Board; and all instances of neglect or refusal shall be reported to the Board. Every application for a leave of

absence by a Clerk, or person in the Bank, shall be made to the President or Cashier, who shall grant or refuse the same as they may deem expedient." Annual vacations had not been discovered at that time, and bankers hours were obviously long ones. The bank was opened for business every day of the year, except Sundays and days recognized by the laws of Tennessee as national or religious holidays. Public business was conducted between 9 a.m. and 3 p.m., but considering the great amount of painstaking record keeping that had to be done by hand, it is obvious that the employees had to work many additional hours. No women were employed. It was contrary to the customs of the time, and men were accustomed to an economy in which laborers worked from dawn to dusk in almost all jobs.

*Early Bank of Commerce passbooks
dated 1874 (closed) and 1893 (open).*

All officers of the Bank of Commerce were required to take the following oath: "I do solemnly swear or affirm, that I will faithfully discharge the trust reposed in me as...of the Bank of Commerce; and that I, will not wilfully or knowingly violate any direction or provision of the Charter of said Bank, nor any By-Laws made for the regulation of the Bank, nor will I disclose to any person the amount of discounts made, the state of the Bank and its funds, or any of the business and transactions thereof, which are not of a public nature, except to individuals who may inquire concerning their own particular business. So help me God."

The Board of Directors regularly maintained a careful supervision of the operation of their institution. A committee, appointed every three months, was responsible for counting the cash on hand, comparing the assets and liabilities with the balance on the general ledger, and determining whether the books were correctly kept to correspond with the condition of the bank. This committee reported to the Board at its next regular meeting. These meetings were held at the bank building on the first Tuesday of each month, although special sessions could be called by the president or the cashier as needed.

All books and accounts were required to be balanced on the first Monday of each month, the day before the regular meeting of the Board. Meetings were called to order by the president, who read a report on the state of the bank, including the balances with other banks, the amount of the income and of the notes and bills offered for discount, and the overdrafts since the previous day. A quorum consisted of a majority of the members of the Board of Directors. Any member had the right to enter upon the record his protest against any action taken at a meeting, with the reasons for his vote, provided that it was expressed in "temperate and respectful language."

The new bank solicited, and soon acquired, accounts from a large number of individual and business customers. Everyone opening an account had to provide certain required information and enter his name in a record called the "Book of Signatures." The president and cashier were directed to close any accounts they considered necessary "for the safety and convenience of the bank," although the reasons for these closures had to be reported at the next meeting to the Board of Directors, which had the authority to accept or reject the actions taken.

The original stock of the Bank of Commerce could be increased when the need for additional capital was agreed upon by the Board of Directors. Further issues

of stock were certain to be needed if the new bank prospered as the founders intended. When a new stock issue was approved, all current stockholders had to be notified, for they had the privilege of subscribing to shares of the new issue in proportion to their holdings of the existing stock. If any stockholders failed to exercise their privilege to acquire shares of the new issue within 60 days, the board had the authority to make it available to other subscribers. New issues of stock were, of course, eventually needed, but the original capitalization of the bank, of $200,000, was not increased during the first 14 years of its operational history. This delay was caused, not by limitations in the management of the bank, but by severe regional and national economic difficulties that the founders of the institution could not possibly have foreseen in 1873.

Indeed, the status of the nation seemed particularly auspicious for the founding of new financial institutions when Edgar McDavitt assumed the first presidency of the Bank of Commerce. The bitter and emotional era of Reconstruction was drawing to a close, and the United States had already entered its greatest period of business growth. Ulysses S. Grant had just been sworn in for his second term as president of the United States, and while he was generally disliked in the South because he was a Republican, financial leaders in all parts of the nation recognized that this party was the champion of business interests. Following the inflation of prices during the Civil War, the government had begun a deflation of the money supply that was to be continued through most of the remainder of the century. This was also an era of unprecedented expansion and consolidation of business.

The banking business benefited from this national economic policy. As the supply of money in relation to the general economy contracted, currency increased in value. While this change was harmful to debtors, it was advantageous to creditors, including financial institutions. According to a financial historian, A. G. Hart, the total money supply in the United States the year the Bank of Commerce was established was only a little more than $2 billion. At this time, according to information provided later by the Federal Reserve System, there were 277 state banks and 1,968 national banks in the United States. The Banking Act of 1864, by establishing the legal framework for a national banking system, had reduced speculative competition and brought stability to the business.

Although the founders of the Bank of Commerce secured a state rather than a national charter, their standards exceeded those of the Federal Banking Act. Their capitalization of $200,000 was twice that of the amount of $100,000 required by federal regulations for cities with a population of more than 6,000 but less than 50,000. And it is doubtful that federal regulations would have required managerial and accounting procedures more rigorous than those they practiced.

When the Bank of Commerce started, the situation in Tennessee government was more troubled, but still favorable toward business to the extent that political leaders had the ability to be of assistance. Following Reconstruction, conservative control was restored by the Democratic party as Tennessee began its century-long experience as a part of the single party system of the Solid South. The Democratic party controlled the state and John C. Brown, a former Confederate general, served as governor. Since the state was still mainly agricultural, this party had only a small faction of "Industrial Democrats" who supported business interests. Because of their financial resources, and the appreciation of state politicians for money, this faction was usually able to direct legislative action on business matters. Brown himself was a strong supporter of business interests. In 1873, he endorsed a funding act that was favorable to bondholders, and later he served as a railroad executive and as president of the Tennessee Coal, Iron and Railway Company.

In Memphis, the economic setting of most crucial concern to the founders of the Bank of Commerce, the situation also seemed encouraging for the beginning of a new financial business. In 1870, the population of the city had grown to a new level of 40,246, and the total

banking capital had increased to $1,700,781. The four existing railroads had been rebuilt, and two new ones were under construction, one to Selma, Alabama, and the other to Paducah, Kentucky. Eleven steamboat lines with 40 boats operated from the city. With a population almost twice the size of either Atlanta or Nashville, Memphis was able to dominate the financing of its large service area.

During the 1870-1871 season, 511,432 bales of cotton valued at $39,552,256 were sold in Memphis. This was almost 12 percent of the total cotton production in the United States. The city led the nation in the production of cottonseed oil, having an annual total of 7,400 barrels. Wealth in the city was demonstrated by palatial homes built on the avenues leading out of downtown by the merchant princes, bankers, and professional men. When the great Chicago fire occurred in 1871, Memphis residents quickly contributed $50,000 to be sent to the victims. The Cotton Exchange and the chamber of commerce worked with the local press, *The Daily Avalanche*, *The Daily Appeal*, and the *Weekly Public Ledger*, to promote commerce and growth.

An attempt to describe the early history of the Bank of Commerce would not be complete without a brief notice of some of the other businesses operating in Memphis at the time. They shared the same trials and opportunities of the city, and some of them throughout the years were to become customers or other associates of the bank. Advertisements and notices from them appeared in the same newspapers, particularly *The Daily Avalanche*, *The Daily Appeal*, and the *Weekly Public Ledger*. These included: B. Lowenstein & Brothers; Stratton-Wellford, with John T. Stratton and John L. Wellford; the Peabody Hotel; Menken Brothers; Schwab & Company; John S. Toof of Toof, Phillips & Co.; Royster, Trezevant & Co., real estate exchange; Hill, Fontaine & Co., with Napoleon Hill, N. Fontaine, and Jerome Hill; W. S. Bruce & Co., carriage makers; Grider & Denie, building supplies; W. B. Galbreath Cotton Ginning; Memphis City Fire & Gen. Insurance Co., with B. Bayliss, W. B. Galbreath,

One of the city's early businesses, D. Canale & Co., was also one of the first customers of the Bank of Commerce. Founded in 1866, the food wholesaler is pictured here at its Front Street home, circa 1907.

Napoleon Hill, and R. B. Goodlett; Mississippi Valley Fire & Marine Insurance, with F. S. Davis, W. A. Gage, R. A. Pinson, H. Seessel, Jr., and F. M. Mahan; H. Seessel, Sr. & Sons; John Gaston Restaurant; Christian Brothers College; F. M. James and Co.; and St. Mary's Boarding and Day School for Young Ladies. Other individuals and businesses were listed, and others would appear throughout the years, but these were some of the advertisers who shared life in the city with the bank at its beginning.

The early history of the Bank of Commerce was characterized by capable management and steady growth of business. Individual and corporate depositors opened accounts, the officers performed their duties carefully, and the Board of Directors maintained a close watch over the operations. The large capitalization of the bank provided a margin of securi-

ty. These resources were needed by the new institution, because in September 1873 it encountered two major disasters: a yellow fever epidemic and a severe financial panic and depression.

The yellow fever struck first. Brought by steamboat from New Orleans, it started in August and by the beginning of September it was spreading through the city. Large numbers of residents, including a majority of the city council, fled the city in fear so that no official business could be carried out during the emergency. Memphis was managed during this time by a temporary committee that included business leaders and ordinary citizens. More than 5,000 people contracted the fever in this year and about 2,000 died before the first frost at the close of October ended the epidemic. A disaster of this size, of course, was sufficient to disrupt all business activities in the city.

One of the businesses to incur loss was the Bank of Commerce which experienced the first death of one of its directors. The local newspaper edition on October 1, 1873, carried the following notice: "Mr. Eugene Magevney, one of our oldest and most universally esteemed citizens, died yesterday at his residence on Adams Street. He had reached the advanced age of seventy-five years, nearly half of which were spent in Memphis. In every relation of life Mr. Magevney's conduct was that which won for him the highest respect of his fellow citizens, and his death will be generally regretted."

The year's second disaster to strike Memphis began far away, in New York and Philadelphia, with the failure of Jay Cooke and Company, one of the largest banking firms in the nation. Cooke had helped to finance the United States government during the Civil War and had then invested extensively in railroads. A substantial part of the great business boom of the early 1870s had been built by speculative bank financing of railroads and industries. The collapse of Jay Cooke and Company caused a general banking panic throughout America.

This panic reached Memphis by September 25, a date described by newspaper accounts the following day as "Black Thursday." *The Daily Avalanche* reported: "Yesterday was a black day in the financial and mercantile affairs of Memphis. The wave of panic that originated in the failure of Jay Cooke & Co., more than a week ago, and caused failure after failure in Eastern financial circles, struck us at last and compelled the suspension of two of our leading institutions, the First National and the DeSoto Bank. Confidence had been shattered and it was evident to those more observing and better informed, that a quiet but steady drain of currency from most, if not all of the banks was in progress. This drain attained the character of a run on Wednesday, and lifted from the First National Bank not less than $61,000 between the hours of 2 and 3 o'clock, which left it in such condition as to render suspension necessary."

The news report of the closing of the DeSoto Bank read as follows: "In the back room of the DeSoto Bank the Avalanchian found Messrs. Elder and Farnsworth, and learned that their deposits which amounted to over $500,000 in June had run down, due principally to the panic, to $190,000, on which they were forced to suspend. They expressed the firm belief that they would soon resume business, the immediate obstacle being inability to procure currency, and that the assets of the concern were ample to discharge full liabilities, the concern having suffered no losses."

The remaining banks in the city had experienced runs by their depositors, but generally experienced less difficulty. Customers of the German National Bank, with a strong loyalty to it, had withdrawn only about $20,000, and it remained solvent. Union and Planters Bank had lost funds during the run, but had been able to secure additional deposits, and thus survived the crisis.

The newspaper included the Bank of Commerce in the list of institutions experiencing least difficulty: "At the other banks, which, if not new concerns, do comparatively a small business, there was less evidence of panic, and the State National (one of the new) closed with a better deposit account than it opened with. All the collections of the First National were turned over to it. There was some run on the Emmet, and rumors concerning it were in circulation last night. Its business is principally among the poorer classes. The Fourth National and Bank of Commerce passed through the ordeal very quietly, as did also the Manhattan and the Mechanics' and Traders', which latter two, however, do principally a brokerage business." There is no doubt that the officers and directors of the Bank of Commerce were pleased that this was one ordeal through which they could pass "very quietly."

Although not included in the news about major banks, there was one other tragic chapter in the history of Memphis banking that took place during this panic. The Freedman's Savings Bank, established during Reconstruction to provide financial aid to citizens of African-American descent during their transition from slavery to freedom, also experienced a run. It suspended operations under the term of the 60-day law. Although it advertised that it had suffered no loss and was solvent, it was never able to reopen for business. The next black-owned bank would not be established until the 20th century had started.

As fear caused by the panic spread through the Memphis business community, a movement was organized to seek special credit assistance from the banks of the city. The chamber of commerce appointed a committee of 10 men to solicit relief from the banks to deal with financial difficulties of the business community. Within one day this committee, having met with officers of all the banks in operation, reported on their efforts to what was described as "the largest assemblage of bankers, merchants and business men which probably ever gathered together before in Memphis." The banks had agreed not to suspend currency payments, but to pay checks of all dealers drawn against their currency balances as usual. The banks also agreed, in a statement that may have been carefully drafted to avoid added liability to themselves, to attempt to help local businessmen in their transactions with the banks outside of the city. A resolution was adopted "that the action of the banks of Memphis meets the hearty approval of the chamber of commerce."

The Bank of Commerce was represented at this meeting, as was the Fourth National Bank, Union and Planters Bank, German National Bank, State National Bank, Manhattan Bank, Mechanics' and Traders' Bank, and Emmet Bank. The possibility that the management of the Bank of Commerce may not have given wholehearted approval to this agreement, secured under such concerted pressure, is suggested by the fact that it was represented at the meeting by neither its president nor cashier, but by the assistant cashier, J. E. Mulford.

The Bank of Commerce may not have pleased all residents of the city who wished to secure concessions of easier credit during the hard times, but it survived the depression, even though it had obviously experienced losses of currency during the run. It did more than just survive; it remained both solvent and profitable. Furthermore, it had one of the greatest successes of its history as a result of this depression.

The DeSoto Bank, a strong institution with deposits of $500,000 when the Bank of Commerce was founded, nevertheless experienced heavy losses during the panic. It was still basically sound, having important business accounts, including that of the Hernando Insurance Company with which it had long been identified. Its directors were so favorably impressed with the strength and stability of the Bank of Commerce through the financial crisis that in 1874 they arranged for the DeSoto Bank to be absorbed into it.

The Bank of Commerce acquired not only the business of the DeSoto Bank, but the services of its vice president, Samuel H. Dunscomb, who became its vice president at the time of the merger. This was a fortunate acquisition for the growing new bank, for he was one of the most successful of Memphis bankers during the century. He was born in Kentucky in 1822, the son of a veteran of the War of 1812. Orphaned as a child, he grew up with very little schooling, but with an unusual amount of intelligence and ambition. He secured his first job, while still a boy, in a general store in Bowling Green, Kentucky. It was there that he began his education in the mercantile business, in which he was to win both success and wealth.

He first came to Memphis in 1846, taking a job with a wholesale grocery and commission business on Front Row, later to become Front Street. He held this position only a year before moving to New Orleans where for another year he served as a clerk in a wholesale dry goods firm. Having learned the business and saved his money, he then moved to Careyville, Arkansas, where he opened a store of his own in this Ouachita River town. He remained there for eight years, but he had never forgotten his experience in Memphis.

He moved back to the Bluff City in 1856 to become a member of the firm of Stratton, McDavitt & Company, wholesale grocers and commission merchants. There he was associated with Edgar McDavitt, with whom he shared many characteristics and interests, and with whom he would serve again, 18 years later when both were officers of the Bank of Commerce. Their mercantile firm was one of the most prosperous in the city until it failed after the federal capture of Memphis in June 1862.

On the same day that Yankee infantry regiments marched into Memphis, Dunscomb left the city. His hegira was like that of the Memphis *Daily Appeal*, also a strong supporter of the Confederacy, which loaded its type and presses into a railroad boxcar and fled southward when the enemy occupied the city. His health was too poor to allow enlistment in the Confederate army, but for three years he traveled through the South, serving the Confederacy as a business agent.

John T. Fargason

In 1865, when the Civil War was over and military occupation of Memphis ended, he returned home like the veterans of the Confederate army. His old firm, Stratton, McDavitt & Company, had been destroyed by the war, but it was reorganized as Stratton, Goyer & Company, with Samuel Dunscomb as a full partner. Despite difficult times, the capable management of this company quickly made it prosperous. He prospered with the firm until 1867 when he retired from it because of poor health. Within a year, however, he had recovered sufficiently to accept the presidency of the Hernando Insurance Company. In 1869, he was appointed president of the DeSoto Bank,

which institution he served until it was taken into the Bank of Commerce.

The management of the new bank continued to be of exceptionally high quality through the remainder of the century. In addition to Samuel Dunscomb, there was another vice president, John Overton, Jr., who was also appointed in 1874. His appointment was announced in February of that year. There is, however, a misconception about the presidency of the bank that should be corrected.

Edgar McDavitt was the first president of the Bank of Commerce when it was organized in 1873. *The Memphis Avalanche* on March 29, 1873, included the following notice: "The officers of the Bank of Commerce elected Thursday are: E. McDavitt, President; J. T. Fargason, Vice President; and R. A. Parker, Cashier." Confusion has arisen over the length of McDavitt's service and the identity of his immediate successor. A number of 20th century accounts, all apparently copied from one another, state that McDavitt served until 1880. Robert Talley's much used and generally excellent account, *80th Anniversary National Bank of Commerce*, published in 1953, stated that Samuel H. Dunscomb became the second president of the Bank of Commerce in April 1880, succeeding Edgar McDavitt.

But according to primary sources from the early years of the bank's history, this account is simply incorrect. *The Memphis Avalanche*, on February 26, 1874, published the following report: "John T.

Fargason has been elected President of the Bank of Commerce, in place of Edgar McDavitt, resigned. John Overton, Jr., succeeds Mr. Fargason as Vice President." A paid notice by the bank in the same newspaper on April 4, 1874, lists J. T. Fargason, president, J. Overton, Jr., vice president, and R. A. Parker, cashier. The members of the Board of Directors were listed in the following order: E. McDavitt, Thos. H. Allen, J. T. Fargason, J. Overton, Jr., Howell E. Jackson, Nathan Adams and O. H. P. Piper. Records of the bank from its first decade are fragmentary, and there might be some possibility that Edgar McDavitt returned later in this period to serve again as president. But if these primary sources are correct, and there is no reason to disbelieve them, John T. Fargason rather than Samuel H. Dunscomb was the second president of the bank, and the date of McDavitt's resignation as president was 1874 rather than 1880.

Regardless of the chronology and sequence of service of its collective officers, it is still obvious that the bank had the advantage of unusually capable management during the era. This strong leadership was needed, for the decade was a troubled one. Memphis suffered from the continuing depression, a heavy municipal indebtedness, and an extraordinary degree of political corruption and incompetence — even for the Bluff City. The fiscal condition of the city continued to worsen through the decade. By 1878 the city treasury was empty, tax collections declined, and employees were told there was no money to pay their salaries. The U.S. Supreme Court ordered the city to pay almost $500,000 to a contractor who had installed the rotting Nicholson pavement. Other creditors quickly secured judgments against the city. The city council began meeting secretly to avoid U. S. marshals with papers to serve. It seemed that things had gotten as bad as they could get, but this was not true. Something much worse was about to happen.

During the summer the greatest disaster in the history of the city approached. By June 3 news had arrived that a yellow fever epidemic had started in the West Indies. Early in July it reached New Orleans, and by the end of the month it had gotten to Grenada, Mississippi. On August 5, 1878, death came to Memphis. Mrs. Kate Bionda, the owner of a downtown restaurant, was the first casualty of the yellow fever. The reaction of other residents then became utter terror and panicked flight. People crowded the railroad stations and steamboat landings and filled roads leading out of the city. By the time the flight was over, about 34,000 of the estimated 56,000 people in Memphis were gone.

Of the 22,000 residents left to face the epidemic, about 7,000 were white and 15,000 were black. An estimated 17,600 of them contracted the fever and 5,150 died. Many businesses and some of the banks, but not all of them, closed. Some of the business closures were permanent. The waterfront was deserted and the city seemed empty except for family members seeking help for the sick and workers removing and burying bodies.

Suffering and death on such a vast scale provided opportunities for heroism, and there were many heroes in Memphis. Political leaders left at the beginning of the epidemic; the citizens relief committee was again formed to run the city and provide relief for the destitute. Clergymen of many faiths, particularly Catholic, remained to minister to the dying. Almost all of the policemen, black and white, served through the epidemic.

Some heroes and heroines appeared unexpectedly. One was Annie Cook, a business woman whose house of prostitution, Mansion House, at 359 Main, provided sex at 50 cents per customer. Touched by the suffering around her, she discharged her girls and opened the house as a hospital. She nursed victims of the epidemic until she became ill herself and died with the fever.

Not all businesses closed. The Bank of Commerce remained open to provide relief funds for victims of the epidemic, although it is probable that it was kept open at reduced hours, as its officers had done during the yellow fever five years previously. C. B. Galloway, the owner of the Peabody Hotel, provided lodging with only two employees left to help him. John Keating continued to publish *The Appeal*, although only two of his 75 employees who did not leave or become ill remained.

By the end of October, cold weather had arrived and the yellow fever was over for the year. Some refugees who had fled began coming back home. Many did not care to return. The economy had suffered massive damage, and the cultural diversity of Memphis was gone. Most of the Germans moved to northern cities; many of the Irish had died. Some of the early families had disappeared. Memphis was not the same city that it was when the Bank of Commerce had been founded.

Despite the magnitude of the disaster, there was still hope for the future of the city. Its population had actually declined during the decade, from 40,246 to 33,592, but former residents gradually began moving back to their homes. More businesses began to be reopened, and all the original physical structures of the city were still intact. The citizens held a meeting in which they approved a proposal to surrender their municipal charter. In 1879, the legislature abolished the corporate charter of Memphis, establishing instead the Taxing District of Shelby County. Thus, as far as the charter was concerned, the city came to an end. Nonetheless, the physical and human components that had made up the city of Memphis the day before the act was passed still remained after its passage. They were then a part of the new entity, "the Taxing District," which possessed everything that Memphis had previously had, except its government. Since this area had no municipal charter, its residents did not have the right of self government.

The General Assembly therefore appointed officials to manage this new district. These men, answerable to the legislature rather than the local residents, were all wealthy and successful members of the area's business community. Their selection gave assurance that the newly designated district would be managed efficiently, and that the city previously called Memphis would be governed in a manner favorable to business. And when the future rebuilding would be undertaken, the successful and solvent Bank of Commerce, having survived plague and depression, would be a major participant.

Having survived the disasters of depression and epidemic, the Bank of Commerce entered the decade of the 1880s with increased managerial and financial strength. The Memphis Mardi Gras Carnival in 1878 celebrated the end of the yellow fever.

CHAPTER FOUR

FINANCIAL LEADERSHIP
DURING A RENAISSANCE OF MEMPHIS

Whm the founding officers and directors of the Bank of Commerce established their institution with such careful calculations and high hopes for success, they could not have realized that the decade would be one of the worst in the history of the city for the beginning of a new business enterprise. The fact that the bank survived the disasters of depression and yellow fever and remained solvent and profitable was a result of their prudent management and strong capitalization. The institution entered the decade of the 1880s with increased managerial strength, including a new president, cashier, and several members of the Board of Directors.

In an election held at the Bank of Commerce on April 13, 1880, the number of members of the Board of Directors was increased to 13. Business considerations rather than superstition obviously governed the decision to increase their membership to this number. The enlarged board included the following men: Thomas H. Allen, cotton merchant; John T. Fargason, J. T. Fargason Company; Samuel H. Dunscomb, DeSoto Insurance Company; E. Lowenstein, B. Lowenstein and Brothers; J. A. Taylor, Taylor and Carroll, attorneys; S. Mansfield, S. Mansfield and Company, drugs; M. Gavin, M. Gavin and Company, wholesale grocers; R. L. Cochran, E. L. Cochran and Company, lumber; Robert Bogardus Snowden, capitalist; John Overton, Jr., Overton and Overton Real Estate; H. Wetter, Wetter Manufacturing Company; W. F. Taylor, cotton factor; and W. B. Mallory, W. B. Mallory and Sons Company.

At this time, the Bank of Commerce also acquired an invaluable addition to its leadership with the selection of its new president. He was Samuel H. Dunscomb, who had served as a vice president of the bank since it had acquired the DeSoto Bank six years previously. A prominent member of the urban business community, he also served as president of the

Hernando Insurance Company, a fire and marine insurance corporation that had been in business since 1850. The board of directors of the Hernando Insurance Company included R. L. Cochran and W. B. Mallory, so there was apparently a close relationship of mutual benefit between the two enterprises. With a paid-up capital of $150,000, the insurance company was also a leading business in the city. Such interlocking directorates were common among major businesses, and doubtless the participation in them by officers and directors of the Bank of Commerce was a great advantage in extending its influence through the community. The insurance company was located at 22 Madison Street, only a few buildings east of his office at the bank. He thus found it a simple matter to move from one business to the other.

The bank prospered steadily under his leadership. He was described in an article on banking in the city in the *Memphis Evening Scimitar* as "one of the most shrewd as well as the most conservative and careful financiers in the city." Active in the affairs of his community, he served for many years as treasurer of the Memphis Board of Education and as a trustee of the Leath Orphan Asylum, which still exists more than a century later as the Porter Leath Child Care Center.

The respect of the other astute businessmen who served as directors with him was such that they reelected him annually as president until his death 18 years later.

John Overton, Jr. continued his service as vice president of the bank. A son of one of the first proprietors of the city, he managed the land holdings that made up the large estate of the family. In addition to his extensive business in general real estate and property rental, he was involved in the insurance business and railroad investment. He had previously served as president of the Tennessee Midland Railroad. Within a year after Dunscomb became president of the bank, Overton was appointed for a two-year term as president of the Shelby County Taxing District. Since Memphis had no municipal charter during this decade, the president of the Taxing District was for all practical purposes the mayor of the city at this time. Overton continued to serve as vice president and director of the bank while he held this public office. Local government during this time, of course, was both efficiently managed and highly favorable toward business and financial interests. In 1889, he and another bank director, W. B. Mallory, joined three other Memphis businessmen, Luke E. Wright, West J. Crawford, and Gilbert D. Raine, to finance a new newspaper, the *Daily Commercial*, which would later merge with *The Daily Appeal*.

Considering the high quality of business experience and managerial ability of the directors and senior officers of the Bank of Commerce, it is difficult to see how

Samuel H. Dunscomb

any financial institution could have entered this era of growth and economic expansion with more capable leadership. But the bank was equally well served by the new employee who became its second cashier, James A. Omberg. He was hired by the Board of Directors in 1879, to serve, under $30,000 bond, as a replacement for the original cashier, Robert Parker, who retired that year.

The important nature of this position was described by an article, published in the *Memphis Daily Appeal*, shortly after Omberg's appointment. The story read as follows: "Bank Cashiers. The Pillars of Memphis Banking. A Record of Seven Busy and Useful Lives. Climbing Up the Ladder of Fortune by Sure Degrees. What Honesty and Fidelity to Duty Will Accomplish. A Lesson to Ill-Advised Young Men Who Favor Quick Methods of Acquiring Fortune — Work Your Way Up.

"The cashiers of the banks of Memphis are as well equipped a class of men as one will find engaged in the banking business anywhere in the world, and it is largely due to their intelligence, financial skill and prudent management that the commercial credit of this city is high and its reputation for financial solvency unsurpassed anywhere. It is gratifying in glancing over the brief record of their lives to note that they are all men who have risen from the ranks, by dint of honesty, industry and faithful application to the duties committed to their care.

"Their lives furnish a valuable lesson to young

men with the world before them, and the lesson is this: That any young man who will apply himself industriously to his chosen vocation in life, act honorably by his fellowmen, avoid bad habits and bad company and live up to the letter of his obligations, is sure to be rewarded with a gratifying measure of success, particularly in a city of such boundless possibilities as Memphis." Although written more than a century ago, this description of the duties and opportunities of bank employees might have some relevance for individuals entering the banking profession today.

A summary of the life of James A. Omberg was included in this feature. Omberg was born at Lawrenceville, Georgia, on October 9, 1839, and attended school at the nearby town of Rome. At the age of 17, he moved to Chattanooga where he began his banking career with a clerical job in the Bank of Chattanooga. In 1857, he moved to Memphis when his bank was consolidated with the Bank of Memphis. He served as a clerk in this bank for the next four years.

When the Civil War began in 1861, the young bank employee joined the Confederate army, enlisting as a private in the Fourth Tennessee Infantry Regiment which was organized at Germantown. His experience during the next four years would have provided a test of the fortitude and endurance of any man. After fighting in most of the major battles of the war in Kentucky, Tennessee, and Georgia, his regiment was surrendered with the army of General Joseph Johnston

James A. Omberg

in North Carolina in 1865. When the Fourth Tennessee was organized, it included almost 1,000 men. By the end of the war, only a few dozen remained.

Returning to his home in Memphis, he resumed his career in banking. His first position, which he held until 1869, was with the Commercial Bank. In that year a new institution, Union and Planters Bank, was organized and he accepted a position there as teller. His competence in this employment brought him to the attention of the men who founded the Bank of Commerce. So when their first cashier, Robert Parker, retired in 1879, James Omberg became his successor.

Although many of the early records of the Bank of Commerce have not survived the passage of time, it is fortunate that some of them remain today, having been preserved through the various moves and changes the institution has experienced. Among them is a collection of miscellaneous papers left by this young Confederate infantry veteran during his service as cashier. These personal and professional items reveal something of the character, ambition, and Horatio Alger-like diligence of this career employee of the bank.

His education when he left his native state at the age of 17 could not have been extensive, and his life as a soldier and banker allowed no further time for schooling, but he had the intelligence to understand the vital importance of being well informed about the society in which his institution functioned. Like other bankers who have seen the necessity of knowledge, he worked steadily in the process of self-education by becoming a voracious reader of newspapers, periodicals, and books.

His papers include a bill, incurred during his first year as cashier, from A. W. Bigelow and Company, general news agents, for magazine subscriptions. The list included *Atlantic Monthly*, *Nation*, *Century*, *Harpers Bazaar*, *Popular Science*, *Scribners Monthly*, and *Fortnightly Review*. His reading was not limited to periodical litera-ture. A bill for $369.50, dated August 22, 1883, from Wills and Wildberger, a Memphis book sup-plier, included many books. Among them were copies of *Webster's Dictionary*, *Baptist Church Directory*,

As Bank of Commerce cashier, James A. Omberg signed numerous bank documents such as these checks dated 1880.

Mark Twain's *Life on the Mississippi*, and Charles Darwin's *Descent of Man* and *Origin of Species*. Two years later his magazine subscriptions included two new publications, *Dial* and *Critic*.

One can picture this ambitious cashier as he labored to acquire the education he never received for-mally, reading late at night by the dim light of candles and oil lamps, later by the flickering rays of gas lights, and after he became cashier, by the glow of the new electric bulbs. There is no doubt that Bank of Commerce was well served by the fidelity and diligence of this dedicated employee. He served the institution with dedication throughout most of his long life, pro-viding continuity and stability of leadership, as other subsequent officers have done, through the history of the bank. As he grew older, his slender, erect figure and

his white hair and beard presented an appearance of trustworthiness and dignity that must have won the respect of customers of the bank. A writer for the *Memphis Daily Appeal* said, "In the financial circles of Memphis there is no more genial gentleman or sounder brain than J. A. Omberg, cashier of the Bank of Commerce."

Realizing the need for a banker to maintain contacts with members of the community he served, he took part in the activities of several fraternal organizations. These groups played a major role in the social and business life of the city at the time. The papers he left contain bills indicating he was a member of the Knights of Honor, Royal Arcanum, and the DeSoto Lodge of F.& A.M. His cultural interest was expressed by membership in the Mozart Society which was active in the city during the 1880s. It is good to note that, like the characters of Horatio Alger, his virtues were regarded by his employers. He prospered to the extent that he was able to be accepted into the society of his adopted city, to care for his family well, and to provide them with edu-cational opportunities that he had not been able to enjoy himself. The greatest achievement of his career came later, after the bank had reorganized under a dif-ferent name, when its Board of Directors rewarded his long and faithful service by electing him to member-ship in their group.

The city of Memphis shared the same hopes and participated in the same growth of prosperity that the

Bank of Commerce did during the decade of the 1880s. Both also participated in the difficulties that remained from their previous disastrous times. There was reason for hope. Surely times could not be worse than they had been. The city's population had declined from 40,226 in 1870 to 33,592 in 1880. This was one of only two decades in the history of Memphis when its population actually declined. The other would not take place for another century — until the 1980s. Thus the city lost 17 percent of its population during the decade when the Bank of Commerce was founded.

Some survivors who had fled were productive citizens who would never come back. Many people from other places were afraid to travel to the city. The great yellow fever epidemic of 1878 was bad enough, but the pestilence had returned the following year. There were 2,000 cases in 1879 and 600 deaths. Although this toll was less than the more than 5,000 deaths the year before, it was enough to increase the fear that Memphis was simply an unusually hazardous place to live.

Memphis was also known as a place where taxes were excessively high. This reputation was well earned in an era when Memphis politicians were more dishonest than usual, even for their city. The charter had been surrendered, the municipal debt repudiated, and life tended to be dangerous and often short. It would be another generation before outside investment in the city would be considered safe.

Despite the losses Memphis had suffered, it refused to die. In fact, the decade became one of rebirth for Memphis, just as it did for the stronger financial institutions in it. Like the mythical phoenix, it assumed new life from the crucible of its disaster.

Legally, Memphis was no longer a city — merely a taxing district of the state of Tennessee — but it still had assets. Its incomparable location on the river bluff was unchanged. It remained the center of the great cotton growing area of the lower Mississippi River. Its buildings and most of its institutions, including the strong banks, remained. Its transportation system continued to operate, and all routes in the Mid-South

still led to the Fourth Chickasaw Bluff. The reluctance of outside capitalists to invest in Memphis was a problem, but it also conferred the advantage to local banks of having less competition for investment in their local area.

Most important, it had citizens and leaders, such as those of the Bank of Commerce, who considered Memphis their home. They refused to leave, and they determined to see their city recover and grow.

Population increase was necessary for the growth of the city. Fortunately, there were people who were attracted to Memphis, even after the plagues and municipal reverses. During the 1880s, another great migration began. The new arrivals included both white and black citizens. The U. S. census recorded an increase of 13,810 black residents of the city during the decade, from 14,896 to 28,706. The white population increased by 17,093, from 18,696 to 35,789. The ratio of blacks to whites remained unchanged from 1880 to 1890 at about 44 percent black and 56 percent white.

The new city that took form in the 1880s was different from the cosmopolitan metropolis of earlier decades. The 31,000 newcomers to the city during this decade were divided racially, but they had much in common. Unlike the earlier immigrants who had brought cultural diversity from the nations of Europe, these newcomers almost all had a similar background. They came to the big city from the rural surrounding areas and small towns of Arkansas, Mississippi, and West Tennessee.

Small farmers, tenants, and sharecroppers, forced off the land by depressed agricultural prices of the late 19th century, had no choice but to move to the cities, including Memphis. They were joined in this migration by young men and women from the small towns. Because they were dependent on agriculture, towns in farming areas entered a period of continuing decline. Besides, life in small towns, although peaceful and idyllic to some residents, has often seemed less exciting to younger people than the attractions of the big city. Memphis was the center of urban attraction in the

Mississippi River valley between St. Louis to the north and New Orleans to the south. A steady stream of immigrants made up of dispossessed agricultural workers and ambitious youth from the Mid-South began a migration into Memphis that has continued to the present.

These newcomers and their descendants shaped the character of the city that began to grow in the last decades of the century. Some of them were men of education and ability who became leaders in business and the professions, just as most of the founders of the Bank of Commerce had done. But the majority of them had only limited education and the ambition to find jobs.

They brought with them from the rural South some common traits that helped shape the character of the city to which they came. They were noted for their hospitality, courtesy in social relations, and friendliness to neighbors and strangers. They were generally hard working, loyal to the traditions of the old South, and militantly patriotic in time of war. Accepting a strict code of morality and honesty in relations with others, they conducted many commercial transactions without written contracts. Houses were often left unlocked and the crime rate, at least in the business community and residential areas, seems to have been quite low. They provided the labor necessary for building the new Memphis.

During this era, the new government was not democratic, since its officers were appointed by the Tennessee General Assembly rather than elected by the voters, but it was efficient and apparently it was much more honest than usual for the city. Those appointed to office under district rule, including John Overton, Jr. of the Bank of Commerce, were business and professional leaders who did not need to use their offices to enrich themselves.

Historians who have written on this period have usually divided into two groups: those who believed that the change in government was a result of the yellow fever epidemic, and those who argued that wealthy property owners used the fever as a chance to end the city government in order to repudiate the municipal debt. There is truth in both views. The devastation by the epidemic is obvious, but there is also no doubt that a large number of major taxpayers considered the city's debt to be a creation of corrupt politicians without benefit to the public, and that they sought an opportunity to repudiate it. The repudiation of this indebtedness was only partially successful.

The debt exceeded $6 million and the issue took a complicated route through the courts. Bondholders, most of whom were apparently New York investors who had bought the paper at a discount, received a decision from the Tennessee Supreme Court in 1881 that lawsuits against the former city of Memphis could be brought against the Taxing District of Shelby County. Deciding to seek a compromise settlement, the legislature created several successive liquidating boards during the next few years. Payment of the various bond issues was negotiated at rates ranging from about 33 cents to 70 cents on the dollar. Even though reduced, the debt had to be paid. Increasing prosperity and careful fiscal control in Memphis made it possible to meet these payments.

The most important work of local government in this era, and the one most necessary to economic growth, was providing improvements in public health and sanitation. Following the great epidemic, the National Board of Health inspected sanitary conditions in the city, and made authoritative recommendations which were accepted and carried out. George E. Waring, Jr., a New York sanitary engineer, was brought to Memphis and empowered to construct a sewer system, which the city had not had before. Within a year he had built 30 miles of sewer lines that resulted in the closing of thousands of outdoor privies.

Business leaders, the Merchants' Exchange, and the city newspapers joined in an effective campaign for street cleaning and garbage collection, tasks that had been neglected through most of Memphis' history. Funds were appropriated, workers were hired, and mule-drawn carts were soon put to work collecting the widespread accumulations of garbage that had littered most city streets.

A satisfactory water system was more difficult to develop. Water lines were laid through the decade, but mud and pollution of the river water they carried made the use of it dangerous. The discovery of a large supply of safe drinking water occurred by accident. Richard C. Graves, the owner of an ice plant near Court Street, decided to have a deep well drilled in the hope of finding clean water for his business. On March 17, 1887, at a depth of 354 feet, the drill reached an underground lake and a stream erupted, spewing water five feet above the surface. Tests proved the water clean and safe for drinking. One of the city's greatest assets had been discovered. Within two years, 52 artesian wells were in use.

At the end of the decade sanitary and public health conditions in the city were better than they had ever been. According to author William Sorrels, 50 miles of sewers and 5,000 water taps were in use. The death rate had declined to 26.5 per thousand. Residents would experience panic and depression again, but the age of the great epidemics was over.

During this era of rebuilding, the growth and increasing prosperity of Memphis was matched by that of the Bank of Commerce. Since the success of the bank was interrelated with that of the city, it is understandable that the bank officers and directors participated fully in efforts for civic improvement. The bank continued to operate from its imposing building at 12 Madison Street. During winter, there were added expenses for heating. A bill, approved by James Omberg, was for $25 for the delivery of 50 barrels of Pittsburgh coal, which at that time could have been brought to the city either by railroad or steamboat.

In summer, there were other expenses, for the bank did not neglect the comfort of its employees, and possibly that of its customers. For example, in June 1879, a bill from Bohlen Huse and Company, "The Memphis Ice Company," was for 200 pounds of "Northern Lake Ice," brought regularly to the city by steamboat. This was an age, however, of rapid technological change, as was revealed by a similar bill four years later, in 1883. The invoice listed the same company with a different name: Bohlen-Huse Machine and Lake Ice Co., "Wholesale and Retail Dealers in Artificial Lake Ice." The recently invented refrigerating machinery had appeared in the city, but customers apparently were not yet ready to believe that machine-made ice was real, hence the dealers felt it necessary to advertise it as "artificial" ice. Other inventions of the industrial age began to appear. Typewriters, having

During the late 1800s, the rebuilding, growth, and increasing prosperity of Memphis was matched by that of the Bank of Commerce as both deposits and customers grew in number. Pictured here are a Bank of Commerce passbook, dated 1902, for D. Canale & Co., and a check drawn on the account in 1915.

been invented in 1867, were beginning to be used in businesses, although no record of their purchase has been found among the bank's papers. The adding machine, patented in 1888, soon came to be widely used. But banks of the time were conservative where newfangled things were involved, and the posting of records continued to be done by hand.

The Bank of Commerce had no lack of borrowers for its funds. Most loans were short-term, generally for less than one year. The interest rate seems to have been at least 10 percent annually. Some money may have been loaned at higher rates, for dividends on bank stock at least occasionally were paid at about 10 percent. Some of the loans, as has been the case in other periods of the bank's history, were bad ones. The surviving records include a packet, "Old Past Due Paper," from the 1870s and 1880s. Loans were secured, of course, but sometimes the collateral proved to be less sound than it might have appeared at the time of the loan.

For example, one note for $5,000 was secured by $10,000 of Memphis City Railroad stock deposited in the bank as collateral security. The failure of this railroad naturally affected the value of its stock. Some loans of the time were secured by warehouse receipts, and these could provide excellent security. Most men in the cotton business operated to a large degree on mutual trust of one another, and cotton bales or other agricultural products stored in the warehouses in the city provided tangible security. When real estate was accepted as collateral, bank officers apparently took the necessary time for travel to inspect it. The records include charges for the hire of horses and buggies from C. H. Brachett and Company, Livery Boarding and Sale Stables.

By the mid-point of the decade, 1885, the Bank of Commerce listed a surplus of $75,000 in addition to its capital of $200,000, and had increased the membership of its Board of Directors. The venerable Oliver Hazard Perry Piper, who had not been included in the newspaper report of directors elected at the beginning of the decade, was again included. The two new directors

were T. B. Trezevant and A. B. Goodbar. Trezevant was the vice president of Gorsuch and Trezevant, a leading mercantile firm, and was the treasurer of the influential Merchants' Exchange. He had been active in bringing several large new business enterprises to the city. Goodbar, a principal with Goodbar Love and Company, a prominent wholesale firm, was also active in the Merchants' Exchange.

In 1885, the Board of Directors had the sad duty of noting the death of their first president, Edgar McDavitt, who died at his home, at the age of 79, after a period of declining health. He was given the tribute "Undisturbed by disaster, undazzled by the spectacular, content with duty."

Two years later, in 1887, the directors of the Bank of Commerce made one of their most important decisions. As a result of the unusual success of their institution and the prospect of even greater growth in the future, they voted to triple the amount of their capital stock, from $200,000 to $600,000. The great success of the bank might have justified this decision at an earlier date, but the directors had learned caution from the previous depression through which they had passed. When they did decide to act, it was done with boldness, and their increase of capitalization was an unusually large one.

According to a history of Memphis financial institutions published the following year by O. F. Vedder, the Bank of Commerce had experienced remarkable growth. Among the 12 banks active in the city, it was third in capital, with $600,000; second in the amount of surplus, with $101,407; and third in deposits, with $1,032,977. The Bank of Commerce had also added two new members to the Board of Directors. They were J. S. Day, of Day, Horton and Bailey, wholesale grocers; and J. Sugarman, an investor and insurance executive. It seems, on the basis of banking information carried in the Memphis *Evening Scimitar*, that there were no more changes in membership of the board during the remainder of the decade.

The last decade of the century began for the Bank

of Commerce with a continuation of the prosperity it had achieved during the 1880s. The continuity of its officers and directors kept the institution under control of men described in the Memphis *Evening Scimitar* as "being in the front rank of Memphis' successful and conservative business men. Under them, the bank has enjoyed brilliant financial success."

Encouraged by the great expansion of business that had followed their previous increase of capital stock, the Board of Directors voted in 1890 to further increase the capital from $600,000 to $1 million. The past profitability and future prospects of the bank fully justified this decision. The dividends on the stock issued had seldom ever fallen below 10 percent. The confidence in the bank was so great that every dollar of the new stock issue was easily placed at the rate of $1.50.

The volume of business of the Bank of Commerce continued to increase, and within a year the total of the surplus and undivided profits had increased to $350,000. Three new members had been added to the Board of Directors by this time. They were D. W. Fly, of Fly and Hobson Company; Godfrey Frank, of Godfrey Frank and Company; and W. E. Love, of Wynn-Love and Company, cotton factors.

Another event of great significance in the financial history of the city took place in 1892 with the founding of the Memphis Trust Company. It was established by John T. Fargason, a member of the Board of Directors of the Bank of Commerce, who at that time was both a past and future president of the bank. There was a close relationship between the two institutions, but they continued under separate management for the remainder of the century. Their eventual merger would provide a later chapter in the history of the Bank of Commerce. Both of these firms operated profitably through the panic of 1893 and the depression that followed it.

For the city of Memphis, the final decade of the century was also one of prosperity and growth. The census of 1890 listed the total population of the city at 64,495. While the officials of the Shelby County Taxing District had led their people through hard times, their very success caused an increasing movement for their replacement. As Memphis grew again into a major city, its citizens demanded their former rights to govern themselves by selecting their own officials. The movement to regain home rule for the city developed slowly until the legislature in 1893 returned the power of electing the mayor, vice mayor, and other officials to the residents. But it was two more years before the legislature returned to Memphis the right to collect its own taxes and determine how its funds should be spent.

Memphis began its new life as a city in good fiscal condition as a result of the strict state controls and the careful management of its taxing district officials. But, because of the city's past record of mismanagement and debt repudiation, many members of the financial community had understandable doubts about the credit of the new government. Fortunately, there were some public-spirited businessmen who were willing to support the city. It is an indication of the progress that had been made in Memphis that the investor who bought the first $1,000 bond issued by the city was Robert R. Church, Sr. A black business leader who had become a millionaire in real estate, he was one of the most respected men in the community by residents of both races. Although race relations of the era involved segregation into two separate societies, one white and the other black, much economic progress had been made by the former slaves who made up almost one half of the population of the city. Business and financial interests provided some of the first opportunities for leaders to work together.

The faith that Church and other businessmen held in their city was justified. Memphis' new government functioned well during the 1890s. Not all the new officials elected in the decade were honest, but business influence was strong and municipal expenditures were handled carefully and conservatively. It seemed, for a time, that Memphis had learned something from its past mistakes.

Residents of the city during this era began to be

able to enjoy new urban amenities that had only recently been developed. Telephones, valued at first for business use, were beginning to appear in homes. Electric lights began replacing the older gas lights, and by 1891 the Memphis Light and Power Company was extending lines through the city. It was during this year that the first electric streetcar was put in service. It was so successful that several competitors began providing this new form of transportation. The lines were consolidated in 1895 as the Memphis Street Railway. The demand for these modern conveniences led to the creation of new corporations to supply them, and the Bank of Commerce was active in financing new businesses during the decade.

This progress had the effect, however, of limiting the increase of population inside Memphis. It became possible for workers to commute from the suburban communities of Raleigh, Lenox, Ingleside, Idlewild, Gladstone Heights, and Madison Heights, all outside the city limits. City leaders would have to address the impact of this suburban growth before the end of the decade.

A significant event in the intellectual history of Memphis took place downtown on April 12, 1893, when community leaders gathered near the riverfront for the dedication of a new institution, Cossitt Library. This building was initiated by a large bequest from a former successful Memphis businessman, Frederick H. Cossitt. An extensive effort by private citizens made it

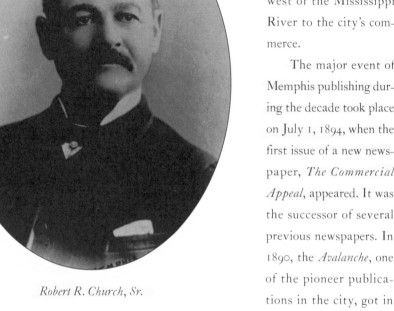

Robert R. Church, Sr.

possible for Cossitt's desire to be carried out. Among the leading supporters were several associates of the Bank of Commerce led by John T. Fargason.

Other major developments illustrated the prosperity of the decade. In 1892, the first bridge across the Mississippi River south of St. Louis was completed. First known as the Memphis Bridge, it later came to be called the Frisco Bridge. It effectively opened a wide area west of the Mississippi River to the city's commerce.

The major event of Memphis publishing during the decade took place on July 1, 1894, when the first issue of a new newspaper, *The Commercial Appeal*, appeared. It was the successor of several previous newspapers. In 1890, the *Avalanche*, one of the pioneer publications in the city, got in financial trouble and was acquired by its even older rival, *The Appeal*. The combined newspaper was published for four years as the *Appeal-Avalanche*. It also soon experienced financial difficulties and was bought by the owners of *The Commercial*, which had been organized in 1889. *The Commercial Appeal* thus began a publishing history which would continue to the present. The owners of this newly formed publishing company were mainly businessmen who were associated with the Bank of Commerce. It is appropriate that the activities of the bank have been regularly reported in this newspaper during the span of almost a century since 1894.

In 1895, the skyline of Memphis began to change. The Dr. D. T. Porter Building, which still stands

Several associates of the Bank of Commerce joined in the effort by private citizens to carry out the bequest of Memphis businessman Frederick H. Cossitt. The result was Cossitt Library on Front Street, opened April 12, 1893.

today, became the first skyscraper to be completed in the city. The invention of the electric elevator and the use of steel girders in building made its construction possible. Thousands of spectators came to see the 11-story structure. The more courageous of them paid a fee of 10 cents to ride the elevator. Other similar buildings would soon follow, but for several years the Porter Building provided the finest view in the city.

The last decade of the century was one of business diversification and financial growth for the city of Memphis. It was also a time of increasing success for the Bank of Commerce. In 1891, Andrew Morrison wrote in the publication, *American City*, "The Bank of Commerce, of 12 Madison Street, with $1,000,000 capital, over $350,000 of surplus and more than $2,800,000 of total resources, is the richest bank in Memphis. It is also the best patronized..."

The Bank of Commerce, like the city of Memphis, continued to maintain a position of financial strength throughout the entire decade. Operations were not suspended and payments were not limited during the panic of 1893. Regular dividends were declared and the bank continued to do business at a profit during the following years. The steady increase in the activity of the bank led to a decision by the Board of Directors to secure a national charter.

Looking south on Main Street at the corner of Madison, 1895.

The charter was granted on January 11, 1897, and the old Bank of Commerce became the new National Bank of Commerce. This new charter and name brought little visible change to the institution. The same experienced officers and directors remained, the original building continued to be used, and the usual business operations earned their traditional profits.

Some changes were required by the regulations governing national banks. The annual election of officers and directors, for example, had to be moved from April to January. The Memphis *Evening Scimitar* on January 11, 1898, reported the following: "National Banks Selected Directors This Morning. Directors Will Choose Officers This Afternoon. All the national banks of Memphis — and they are five in number, the State National, the National Bank of Commerce, the First

National, the Continental National and the Memphis National — are holding elections today, at which directors to serve the ensuing year will be chosen.

"This is in accordance with the federal law which requires that all national banking institutions hold such elections on the second Tuesday in January." The directors elected at this meeting were: John W. Dillard, S. H. Dunscomb, J. T. Fargason, M. Gavin, E. Lowenstein, W. E. Love, W. B. Mallory, Austin Miller, J. A. Omberg, John Overton, Jr., O. H. P. Piper, Robert Bogardus Snowden, and D. T. Porter.

Although the newly designated National Bank of Commerce operated with continuing success through the remainder of the century, it experienced a serious loss on August 28, 1898, when its president during the previous 18 years, Samuel H. Dunscomb, died while on a trip to North Carolina. His sound financial judgment and encyclopedic understanding of Mid-South business had been a great asset during the rapid growth of the bank.

The Board of Directors adopted the following resolution: "We have lost a faithful and honorable executive officer. . .as a banker and a business man his name has always been the synonym for reliability and commercial honor. In losing S. H. Dunscomb we lose an associate whom we all valued as a friend and whom we always found a safe member in times of emergency. But it is not only as a sound and upright business man that the memory of S. H. Dunscomb will be treasured: his private virtues were all the more estimable because they were free from selfish display or the desire for notoriety. The National Bank of Commerce has lost an invaluable officer and Memphis has lost a loyal friend and invaluable citizen."

The Board of Directors elected John T. Fargason to replace S. H. Dunscomb as the president of the bank. As one of the founders of the original Bank of Commerce, Fargason had served as a director since its beginning. He also had previous experience as its president, having served during the 1870s after the resignation of Edgar McDavitt. His business experience was apparently even more extensive than that of Dunscomb. He was the founder and president of the Memphis Trust Company, the resident vice president of the American Surety Company of New York, and a director of many of the larger businesses in Memphis. He provided the continuity of leadership to guide the National Bank of Commerce into the 20th century.

The Bank of Commerce Building, 12 Madison Street, circa 1899.

Looking east on Madison Street from Front Street, circa 1907. The Bank of Commerce building's tower can be seen at left.

CHAPTER FIVE

PROGRESS AND CHANGE
IN A NEW CENTURY

Both National Bank of Commerce and the city of Memphis entered the 20th century in a period of growth and favorable prospects for the future, although the progress of the bank had surpassed that of the city during the previous decade. Under the leadership of its experienced corps of officers and directors, the bank had achieved an even higher level of success after the recent acquisition of its national charter. Its reorganization as a national bank had included a capital stock of $600,000.

A newspaper summary of Memphis banking at the time described it as "one of the strongest banking institutions of this city." The officers at the time were: J. T. Fargason, president; Oliver Hazard Perry Piper, vice president; James A. Omberg, cashier; and Mrs. P. S. Smithwick, assistant cashier. One significant change was noted with the beginning of the new century: Mrs. Smithwick was the first woman to be listed as an officer of the bank, although others would follow her in the years ahead.

Cashier James A. Omberg was serving as a director at this time. There were three new directors: Paul Dillard, of Dillard and Coffin, cotton products; J. T. Fargason, Jr., with J. T. Fargason and Company, wholesale grocers; and Bem Price of Oxford, Mississippi. Apparently the first director appointed outside of the city, Price's affiliation was not listed, but quite likely it was a cotton business. The remaining directors were: J. T. Fargason, Godfrey Frank, M. Gavin, E. Lowenstein, W. E. Love, W. B. Mallory, John Overton, Jr., and Robert Bogardus Snowden.

National Bank of Commerce listed assets and liabilities of $5,206,162.78. The list of assets included: loans and discounts, $1,809,520.61; United States bonds, $800,000; other bonds, $238,787.50; due from U. S. treasurer, $25,000; banking house, $30,000; and

sight exchange and cash on hand $2,302,854.67. The list of liabilities included a surplus of $100,000 and undivided profits of $70,856.46, in addition to the capital of $500,000. Circulation was listed at $500,000, and $18,750 was kept in the fund for taxes. The total amount of deposits was $4,016,556.32. While comparative figures from the other banks in the city are not available for the same date, this total of deposits might have been the highest of any bank in Memphis.

The condition of the city was also favorable at the beginning of the century, even though several political and social problems had begun to appear. Control of government having been returned to the local voters, politics had returned to the inefficiency and corruption that was traditional for Memphis. A problem had also developed in the drive to secure a higher ranking in size among American cities. During the latter part of the 19th century, the Bluff City had fallen behind several of its competitors in the region. The organization of an efficient urban transportation system had initiated a trend that would continue through the 20th century — a continuing growth of suburban communities at the expense of the inner city.

Preliminary surveys indicated that the U. S. census of 1900 might find that Memphis had not only failed to surpass other regional cities, but might actually have lost population. Many people had moved into the city during the decade, but possibly in smaller number than those moving out. The idea occurred to business and political leaders that if enough people had not moved inside the city limits during the decade, the boundaries could be moved out to take them in. ✳

So the year before the census was due, Memphis passed an annexation act. Expanding to the south and the north, but mainly to the east, the city took in 12 square miles. This area annexed was about three times the previous size of the entire city. The plan was successful. It brought in possibly more than 50,000 new residents, both willing and unwilling. Memphis thus began the new century with a population of 102,320 residents. The local newspapers proudly announced that their hometown had passed Atlanta, Richmond, and Nashville in the ranking of Southern cities. Municipal political leaders had also learned an efficient method of creating the appearance of city growth. The future history of Memphis would be a succession of new annexations, usually made shortly before a census was due.

Looking east on Madison Street from Front Street (the same scene as shown in the photograph on page 56), circa 1912. Note modernizations such as the advent of the trolley.

 Of this population total, 52 percent were white and 48 percent were black. In Shelby County, the population had grown to 153,557, of which 55 percent were black and 45 percent white. Of great importance to the growth of Memphis was that the population density of the hinterland surrounding the city — Mississippi,

Arkansas, and West Tennessee — had also increased. This assured an ongoing migration of new urban residents, for the progress of the city depended on continuing to attract the young and the poor of the Mid-South. The great exodus from country to city held steady during the early decades of the century. In 1918, a bulletin of the National Board of Education reported that 4 percent of the black parents and 2 percent of the white parents surveyed in Memphis had been born in the city. Most were born elsewhere in the Mid-South.

The new area of the city included 16 square miles, its street limits being marked approximately by the present location of the Mississippi River, South Parkway, East Parkway, and North Parkway. These streets were laid out at the time around the edge of the area included in the city limits. Within these boundaries, Memphis was beginning to look like a city. In addition to the Porter Building and Cossitt Library, the downtown included the Federal Building, the Tennessee Club, the Grand Opera House, the Lyceum Theater, the Appeal Building, the Cotton Exchange, and the Tennessee Trust Building — now known as the 81 Madison Building. Others were soon to appear, such as the Goodwyn Institute Building and the Memphis Trust Company Building which would be the next home of National Bank of Commerce.

There were a number of hotels, most of them

Main Street at Madison Street, circa 1912.

small, but the two larger ones were the Peabody Hotel and the Hotel Gayoso. The Peabody was built in 1869, four years before the founding of the Bank of Commerce, and was owned until 1953 by the Snowden family, members of which also served as directors of the bank. One of the most historic hotels in Memphis was the Gayoso. It had several fires and closings through the years after its opening in 1842. A fire destroyed it in 1899 but it opened again in 1903. Its ballroom, lobby, dining room, and 400 guest rooms made it the leading hotel in Memphis and one of the grand hotels of the South during its time. The Bank of Commerce was involved in various financial transactions with it.

The economy of the city, although beginning to become more diversified, was still dominated by cotton. The profitable production and distribution of the staple required a large credit supply which continued to absorb much of the available capital of the financial institutions. Cotton men were still involved as officers and directors of the major banks. There were some disturbing signs in the cotton industry at the beginning of the century. The boll weevil had appeared in the United States in 1892 and was beginning to spread. Crop prices remained low and sometimes fell below 10 cents per pound during the decade. However, the volume of the cotton trade in Memphis was so large that it continued to keep the city prosperous. *The Commercial Appeal* reported on October 31, 1900, that 596,945 bales had been sold in the city during the crop season just completed. The value was estimated to be $23,215,191. Since the total production in the United States was 9,436,416 bales, about one out of every 16 bales produced in the nation was sold in the Bluff City.

Every fall during cotton picking season, prosperity came to Memphis. From the fields of the Mid-South, the white fiber arrived. Warehouses were filled and bales were stacked on unused lots along the riverside and on the sides of miles of streets. When it was sold, it was shipped mainly by railroad although steamboats still carried a large amount. Every bale that was sold produced money to be shared by the city and countryside. When the annual crop went to market, cash flowed into the city and out to the plantations. Debts were settled, banks received principal and interest, purchases were made, and money circulated. It was a traditional economy, determined by the seasonal cycle of cotton. There were probably no people in the city who could see that its decline had already started.

The diversity of the Memphis economy was evident in several other areas in addition to cotton. Merchandising throughout a regional distribution market had grown in importance. A newspaper report of the time said: "Excepting from cotton, probably the greatest commercial fame of the city has sprung from her very heavy distribution of supplies of all characters, and in the list of the lines included in this groceries come first. For two miles Front Street is lined with the wholesale houses which have done so much for the city, and the firms owning which have been financially strong enough to carry the planters of Mississippi, West Tennessee, and Arkansas through all the hard times." Principals in the major wholesale firms had been active as stockholders and directors of National Bank of Commerce.

A similar newspaper account described another recently developed business activity: "While removed from the tobacco-producing belts of the South, Memphis enjoys the distinction of being the largest snuff jobbing point in this country, which, of course, means the largest jobbing snuff market in the world." Changing social customs that have led to such a drastic decline in the use of snuff make it difficult for people to realize now what a great popularity this product

had early in the century.

The same newspaper account that heralded the city's status as the largest inland cotton market in the world also gave a favorable account of the rapidly developing timber products. It said, "Lumber alone brings very nearly as much money into the city as cotton. Memphis is the largest hardwood market in the world. She is the second largest lumber market in the world."

It seems that the entire banking community of the city began the century in at least a reasonably prosperous condition. There were six state and national banks with a total listed capital of $3,500,000. In addition to these mercantile banks, there were seven savings banks with more limited assets. Their total capital was only about $300,000. There were also six local, home-owned and -managed fire insurance companies with an aggregate capital of about $1 million. The designation, Queen of the Valley, began to appear in use in the city "not only from a commercial standpoint, but because of her financial institutions."

In an account entitled "The Story of Memphis," *The Commercial Appeal* included the following summary: "One of the greatest attractions to Memphis from a commercial standpoint is found in her financial institutions. She has six state and national banks. And all of them are not only strong and wealthy, but they carry in their vaults enough money to furnish the business men of the city the current cash with which to handle the cotton crop, the lumber product, the grain business, and conduct her manufactories, as well as supply the demand of her wholesale and retail merchants in every line." This description, even if some promotional bias is possible, certainly represented a great improvement from the early days of banking in the city when capital was so scarce it was almost unobtainable.

Apparently this favorable report was essentially true. By 1903, the same newspaper was able to provide additional good news about the local banking community. It said, "For the first time in the whole history of Memphis financial institutions money was loaned out

At the turn of the century Memphis was the world's largest hardwood market and second largest lumber market.

by the local banks to the great banking concerns of New York City. New York is generally considered the center of the financial world, and so it is. At the same time there are conditions prevailing there that under a certain set of circumstances lead to a financial stringency in the money market, or in other words a dearth of actual cash. It is in such times as these that the call loan and time loan rates go soaring upward and it was in such a juncture that several of the Memphis banks, having a surplus of deposits, found it profitable to make a deal with the New York concerns."

National Bank of Commerce by this time had grown rapidly to its position of leadership among the city's financial institutions. The newspaper described it as "one of the strongest props to the rapidly upbuilding commerce and varied industrial interests of the city and its tributary agricultural growth. It is managed by an executive, aided by an influential directorate that is individually known throughout Tennessee and the vast section named as financiers and business men of the highest reputation."

The management of National Bank of Commerce was unchanged, but there was one new director. R. Brinkley Snowden had joined his father, Robert Bogardus Snowden, as a member of the Board of Directors. The assets and liabilities of the bank had increased substantially — to $6,115,209.79. There was still a total of $800,000 in United States bonds, but the amount in other bonds had been reduced to $136,533.33, possibly as a result of more favorable rates on loans. Loans and discounts had increased to $2,629,707.36. But it was in the total of deposits that the bank had made a remarkable gain — to $4,924,603.38. Apparently this amount surpassed that of all other banks in the city. First National Bank listed deposits of $2,609,924.40, and Union and Planters

Bank had deposits of $2,233,107.90. The capital of Union and Planters Bank was $600,000, which was larger than the $500,000 capital of National Bank of Commerce. Union and Planters Bank, however, had no listed surplus, while National Bank of Commerce had $100,000.

During these years, while providing capital for the various new businesses being developed in the city, the bank officers continued their tradition of supporting the agricultural activities of the Mid-South. Large plantation owners were beginning to diversify their crops beyond the traditional reliance on cotton. Warehouse receipts accepted as collateral from the Memphis Elevator, Williams-Fitz-Hugh Company, included one for 4,543 bales of timothy hay weighing 406,855 pounds and another for 2,000 sacks of wheat bran weighing 200,000 pounds. It is evident that the officers of the bank had to remain aware of the value of agricultural products.

A fact about Memphis history that seems unusual today is revealed by these warehouse receipts. They carried a disclaimer stating, "Loss or damage by Riot or Insurrection, Fire, Water, Ratage, Leakage, Shrinkage, Frost or change of weather, or from the inherent qualities of the property, or from being perishable, at owner's risk." Most of these dangers listed are understandable today, but the word "ratage" is unknown to most modern readers. The term was quite familiar to Memphis residents at that time. It had not

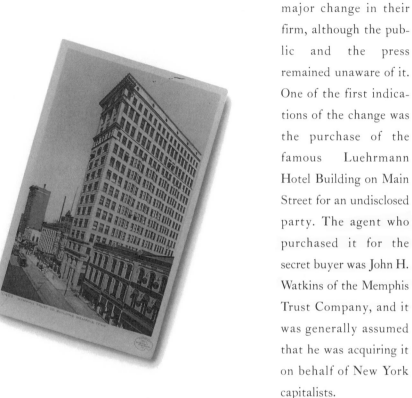

This picture postcard, copyright 1906, shows the Memphis Trust Company building at 14 South Main Street.

been many years since the local newspapers had included stories about the "thousands of rats" that any pedestrian could see during a walk within several blocks of the Peabody Hotel.

By 1904, the officers and directors of National Bank of Commerce were beginning to consider a major change in their firm, although the public and the press remained unaware of it. One of the first indications of the change was the purchase of the famous Luehrmann Hotel Building on Main Street for an undisclosed party. The agent who purchased it for the secret buyer was John H. Watkins of the Memphis Trust Company, and it was generally assumed that he was acquiring it on behalf of New York capitalists.

On May 18, 1904, *The Commercial Appeal* announced that the new owner of the hotel was actually National Bank of Commerce. The bank, which had opened at one of the most impressive buildings in the city, had once again acquired a structure of fame and opulence, at a cost of $120,005 at a chancery court sale. Henry Luehrmann had operated one of the most famous establishments of Memphis at this site. A Union army veteran who had been stationed in the city during the Civil War, he returned in 1866 and became wealthy in the brewing business. Using the fortune acquired as the local bottler and dealer in Schlitz beer, he opened a magnificent restaurant.

Historian Paul Coppock said, "He was the champion of German cooking against the French cuisine of

John Gaston in his small but renowned hotel on the south side of Court Square. Both served finer food than had ever been known in Memphis. As long as the generation who ate at Luehrmann's and Gaston's lived, it was often said that none who came after equalled them."

Although Luehrmann's health had declined and he had experienced financial difficulties by the time the building was sold, Memphis residents had only favorable memories of it. The restaurant was known, "to the upper crust of sportsmen, actors, opera singers, and financiers — as a splendid place to dine in leisure. There were 135 kinds of wine. When the super-rich who traveled in private railroad cars were here for the Memphis Gold Cup season at the Memphis Driving Park or the Tennessee Derby at Montgomery Park, it took five bartenders, plus two lesser figures, to handle the beer drinkers, and to keep the barroom as neat as Luehrmann demanded, even then the crowds were crushing."

The acquisition of this noted building gave National Bank of Commerce some much needed space. Its business had grown so much that the original headquarters on Madison Street became inadequate. During 1903, the bank had paid for alterations of the Madison building and the construction of an addition to provide more space, but even these proved to be inadequate for the bank's needs.

According to a newspaper account, it was still found that, "these quarters are entirely too cramped. It is impossible to enlarge them more, and the directors recognized that it was essential for the bank to purchase other quarters. Increased money demands, increased business ventures by its depositors, and the general growth and enlargement of the commerce of the city, with which the bank is in close touch, disturbed the satisfaction that existed by crowding to the doors employees and customers."

But there was a greater significance to the purchase of this particular building that was known only to a limited number of insiders within the banking community: The property was adjacent to that owned by the Memphis Trust Company. Speculation by local newspapers was concerned mainly with the fact that this new location of National Bank of Commerce moved the financial center of the city from Madison to Main Street.

The story carried by *The Commercial Appeal* said that, "The Memphis Trust Company and the Bank of Commerce are two separate and distinct institutions, just as individual and separate as it is possible for them to be as financial concerns, still, heavy owners of the stock of the bank are also large owners of the stock in the trust company. The Luehrmann Hotel property adjoined the lot on which the Memphis Trust Company will shortly erect its 10-story skyscraper, thus the two institutions, that enjoy such a community of ownership, will be within easy speaking distance." In retrospect, however, it is evident that the members of the interlocking directorate of these two firms were considering more than just a speaking relationship between them.

During 1905, work continued on the new skyscraper commissioned by the Memphis Trust Company. There is some uncertainty as to the architectural firm involved. It may have been designed by the noted Chicago architect, Daniel Burnham who included in his list of commissions in 1904 one from the Bank of Commerce and Trust Company. Some authors have considered this listing to be incorrect, because there was no such company at that time. However, there was to be such a company the following year, and it is possible that this institution existed in the minds of its founders a year before it was officially made public. In addition to the interlocking ownership of stock, it should be remembered that John T. Fargason, the current president of National Bank of Commerce, was also the founder and principal officer of the Memphis Trust Company. Reflecting the financial prominence of the men who built it, the new tower was one of the most impressive buildings in the city at the time. It included 15 floors above ground level. Featuring strong, two-story Ionic columns at the entrance, it was built with rectangular windows to the 11th floor, which changed to arched windows. Above the 12th floor, the order was changed to include Corinthian columns. Its appearance was enhanced by dental molding and parapet work with a wide cornice at the top. It was the most impressive headquarters for a financial institution of the era.

As the building neared completion during the fall of 1905, its actual intended purpose was made public. A public announcement on October 20 of that year revealed the consolidation of National Bank of Commerce and the Memphis Trust Company with the new institution to begin operations in the building nine days later. The bank surrendered its national charter in order to make the change and the trust company applied on October 19 for an amended charter to govern the operations of the new firm. The name of the newly consolidated firm was the Bank of Commerce and Trust Company.

Commemorative silver pocketknife marking the $2 million mark in capital and surplus for the Bank of Commerce and Trust Company, circa 1905.

The total capital stock of this institution was impressive for Memphis at the time. The Memphis Trust Company, which had started with a capital stock of $200,000, had experienced steady growth and had expanded its capital to $1 million after acquiring the Title and Guaranty Company. National Bank of Commerce added $500,000 of capital, giving the new institution a total capitalization of $1.5 million. It also listed a surplus of $500,000.

The Board of Directors of the Bank of Commerce and Trust Company consisted of 20 members, including 15 members previously serving and five men

recently appointed. The new members of the consolidated firm were James A. Omberg, O. C. Armstrong, J. T. Harahan, W. B. Mallory, and W. G. Thomas. The officers were: J. T. Fargason, president; John H. Watkins and J. A. Omberg, vice presidents; P. S. Smithwick, cashier; J. H. Fisher, secretary; W. R. Steward, treasurer; and S. J. Shepherd, trust manager.

Throughout the long history of the bank, its various acquisitions and mergers have generally resulted in the gain of something beyond accumulated financial assets. They have also brought new personnel, some of whom have been among the most faithful and diligent employees of the institution. The consolidation with the Memphis Trust Company brought the first trust officer of the bank, Stonewall Jackson Shepherd.

The character and integrity of "Stoney" Shepherd, as he was known all his life, provided an example of rectitude for all his successors who have served as officers in the trust department of the bank. During a long life that lasted until the World War II era, he devoted his efforts entirely to the bank and its customers. He was remembered long afterward with great respect by all who knew him. Attorney Benjamin Goodman, whose association with the bank spans more than 60 years, remembers him still, in 1993, as a banker of uncompromising principle. Later in life it was necessary for him to work with the assistance of a hearing aid. When any matter required his action, he insisted on learning every possible fact available about it. Once he had made a decision, however, he would remove his hearing aid, and would listen to nothing further on the subject.

The Bank of Commerce and Trust Company, with its strong capitalization and experienced officers, began its operation as a newly named institution by entering another era of growth. It experienced a major loss on January 10, 1909, with the death of its president, John T. Fargason. His death at the age of 74 ended a career of more than half a century as one of the most successful business-men of the city.

The bank's directors honored his long service in a memorial resolution that said, "He achieved an honorable success in the commercial life of a growing city ... he never wronged any man ... he was a true friend a devoted husband and father, and a gentleman of the old school." His

A Bank of Commerce and Trust Company brochure, circa 1905, highlights the bank's financial performance, management team, and services offered.

obituary paid tribute to his business success, but also noted another aspect of his life that was less well known. It said, "Mr. Fargason's pleasure may be said to have been taken from his farms. He had large plan-tation holdings in Mississippi, where he grew cotton under the most scientific farming methods. His pride, however, was probably the Eylau stock farm in Lauderdale county, which is one of the show places of Tennessee. On the Eylau farm stock of the best blood has been raised by Mr. Fargason for many years."

The loss of John T. Fargason left the Bank of Commerce and Trust Company with the necessity of

once again selecting new senior leadership, the first such change in the 20th century. Although not formal-ly named to the position, R. Brinkley Snowden immediately agreed to temporarily accept the duties of the president until the Board of Directors could take official action to make arrangements for continu-ing management. As one of the best known busi-nessmen in the city, Snowden had the man-agerial experience and public respect to assure customers that the bank was in capable hands. A major real estate devel-oper, he had recently opened the Annesdale Park subdivision, one of the most successful projects in the area. His Memphis Hotel Company owned the Peabody and Gayoso hotels, and soon after-ward would construct another, the Chisca Hotel. Members of his family have served as directors of the bank through most of its history.

It was fortunate that a man of Snowden's stature was available for guidance through a critical time, for the bank had recently lost its most experienced officer. James A. Omberg, after a long life of service, had finally left his old bank. Although the different banks in the city were business competitors, there was a degree of friendship and respect among their various officers and directors who made up the banking community. When the directors of First National Bank found it necessary to select a successor to their long time president, C. W. Schulte, they offered the position to Omberg. This offer was apparently made with the approval of the directors of the Bank of Commerce and Trust Company, and it was with their blessing that he left the bank he had served so long to become a bank president. He remained in this position with First National Bank for several years until, at the age of 81, his health began to fail and he gave up the presidency but was made chairman of the board of directors, which office he held until his death several months later.

R. Brinkley Snowden, who had many other business activities to manage, had no interest in serving as the president of the Bank of Commerce and Trust Company. Reportedly, shortly before John T. Fargason's death, he called Snowden to his home and said, "Brinkley, I want you to head the Bank of Commerce." Snowden replied, "No, Mr. Fargason, I won't do that, but I tell you what I will do. You make Tom Vinton president and I'll be vice president and we will run the bank together." After Fargason's death, the directors accepted Snowden's offer to serve as vice president, but apparently they were not yet ready to place Vinton in the president's position.

Instead they turned to Oliver Hazard Perry Piper, the last of the small group of men who had founded the Bank of Commerce 36 years before. Thus at the age of 71 the venerable Piper was called from semi-retirement to serve as interim president of the bank. Born in Maryland in 1838, he arrived in Memphis at the age of

21 in 1859. He started as a construction workman, but within two years, when the Civil War started, he had his own business as a building contractor. He enlisted in one of the first volunteer companies formed in Memphis, the Southern Guards commanded by Captain James Hamilton. They left for camp at nearby Randolph, Tennessee, where they were taken into the 154th Tennessee Regiment. Piper served throughout the war as an artilleryman.

Returning to Memphis after the war, this young combat veteran demonstrated the instincts of a capitalist. He never worked as an employee for anyone else again. Forming his own construction company, he began to secure larger and larger contracts. He did extensive railroad construction over a wide area, and many of the major business establishments built along Front Street were his work. A leading stockholder in the Bank of Commerce, he expanded his business operations into Alabama where he became a leading developer of the coal mining resources of that state. Piper coal carried his name many years afterward. He became one of the richest men in Memphis, which he always claimed as home, although he maintained a summer home at Lake George, New York, and a winter home in Florida. His term as interim president lasted 17 months, until his resignation on June 4, 1910, although he continued to serve the bank as a director for the next 17 years, until his death at the age of 89.

Robert Bogardus Snowden, father of R. Brinkley Snowden and the first of a long line of Snowdens whose association with the bank continues today.

By the time of Piper's resignation as president, the directors were ready to accept R. Brinkley Snowden's earlier recommendation to appoint Thomas O. Vinton as president. Born at Marietta, Ohio, in 1864, nine years before the Bank of Commerce was established, Thomas Oliver Vinton attended Marietta College and began a career in busi-

ness that brought him to Memphis in 1890 as the resident manager of R. G. Dun and Company of St. Joseph, Missouri. He soon accepted a local business position with Barron G. Collier in the gas street lighting business and the gas mantel manufacturing business. Collier left Memphis and later became best known as the advertising tycoon who developed south Florida, but Vinton stayed in the city where he entered the real estate business with R. Brinkley Snowden, who needed a

Thomas O. Vinton

young associate of Vinton's ability. A principal in many of the development projects in Memphis, he won widespread respect by his education, sound business judgment, and obvious intelligence. He was elected president of the Merchants' Exchange and had a street, Vinton Avenue, named for him.

The two business associates, Thomas O. Vinton and R. Brinkley Snowden, obviously worked together as a successful management team for the Bank of Commerce and Trust Company. A surviving statement, dated December 31, 1910, revealed that assets and liabilities had increased to $12,411,834.02, and net earnings during the previous six months, after expenses and taxes had been paid, totaled $399,460.48. Loans

and discounts were listed at $6,582,834.02, and cash and sight exchange included $4,434,763.64. The capital stock remained at $1.5 million but there was $500,000 in surplus and $161,518.87 in undivided profits and contingency funds. The amount of deposits had grown to $10,012,414.93, and, while comparative figures from other banks are not available, it may well be that this was the largest deposit total of any financial institution in the city.

President Vinton was aided by two vice presidents, R. Brinkley Snowden and E. L. Rice. The other officers were: L. S. Gwyn, assistant cashier; James H. Fisher, secretary; G. A. Bone, auditor; and S. H. Shepherd, trust officer. The list of directors included: J. T. Harahan, E. Lowenstein, R. Brinkley Snowden, E. L. Rice, T. O. Vinton, R. A. Speed, P. P. Van Vleet, O. C. Armstrong, W. B. Mallory, B. B. Beecher, John T. Fargason, Jr., T. H. Tutwiler, Cleland Smith, James Nathan, and H. H. Maury.

Under this leadership, the business of the bank continued to grow steadily. The extent of its growth was demonstrated by a story published in *The Commercial Appeal* on May 12, 1912, that the Bank of Commerce and Trust Company had announced the building of a new skyscraper that would double the size of its existing structure. With this announcement, the wisdom and foresight of the bank officers and directors who had bought the old Luehrmann Hotel property eight years before became apparent. Even before the merger of the two banks, they had anticipated that the growth of the consolidated institution would be so great that the large Memphis Trust Company building would not be able to contain it.

Held in readiness for this need, the Luehrmann building had been leased to a group which operated it under the name of the Baumgarten Hotel. The bank exercised its option to cancel the lease so that the building could be demolished in preparation for the new construction. An opening date of September 1, 1913, was scheduled. Since only the lower floors would be used for banking operations, plans were announced to rent the upper levels for office use. So great was the popularity of this location that the bank was able to announce that requests for almost all the available space had been received even before demolition of the old building was started.

Plans for the new tower were drawn up by the architectural firm of Hanker and Cairns. The construction cost was $500,000, all taken from the bank's surplus fund. Connected directly to the original building from its two basement levels through its 15 floors above street level, it was a mirror image of the old structure. Like the original building, it had a frontage of 36.75 feet on Main Street and extended back 148.5 feet to Maiden Lane. The new tower, however, had two basement floors to be opened for rental because, with significant foresight, the original machinery and batteries had been designed to handle the needs of a building

A picture postcard, circa 1920, shows 14 South Main Street as the renovated home of the Bank of Commerce and Trust Company. Known today as the Commerce Title Building, the two towers appear on casual inspection to be a single edifice all of which was constructed at the same time. It is only on close examination that the seam where they are joined is noticed.

twice the size of the one in which they were installed. Known today as the Commerce Title Building, the two towers appear on casual inspection to be a single edifice all of which was constructed at the same time. It is only on close examination that the seam where they are joined is noticed. This building would serve as the home of the Bank of Commerce and Trust Company for the next 16 years.

During this era of rapid growth and prosperity of the Bank of Commerce and Trust Company, there were national banking problems that led to action by the federal government. The panic of 1907, which seems to have had little effect on the more isolated and parochial financial community of Memphis, caused the passage of the Aldrich-Vreeland Act which provided for an investigation of the monetary system. Needed reforms, though, were delayed until after the Democratic party won control of the presidency and Congress in 1912. An important part of Woodrow Wilson's New Freedom was the Federal Reserve Act, passed on December 2, 1913.

This act provided for the establishment by the federal government of a system of 12 regional banks. Although owned by the private banks in each district, their policies would be set by the Federal Reserve Board. They provided the banking system with a lender of last resort. National banks were required to join the system, but it had no control over state-chartered banks. Since the Bank of Commerce and Trust Company had surrendered the charter of National Bank of Commerce at the time of their merger, the officers and directors had the option of remaining outside of the Federal Reserve System until they wished to join. By 1918, they had become convinced that the benefits outweighed the disadvantages and the bank joined the system.

Both the city of Memphis and the bank completed the second decade of the 20th century and entered the 1920s in a generally prosperous condition. The two major developments of the previous decade that affected the nation and the city had been the strong expansion of governmental power by President Woodrow Wilson's New Freedom and the American participation in the first World War. These two factors had brought national economic prosperity, although the explosive growth of wartime had brought a sharp inflationary increase of prices. This produced a much needed rise in agricultural prices which was advantageous to the institution which had become the leading lender to the cotton industry — the Bank of Commerce and Trust Company.

As Memphis began the new decade, its population had grown to 162,351, although the percentage of increase was lower than in any of the previous four decades. The city had continued its policy of annexation. Just before the census was due, Memphis had added territory around the parkways. The most important part of this newly acquired land was the previously independent town of Binghampton.

The Twenties, more than any earlier decade, brought a rebellion against traditions and a search for new activities. The era acquired its own symbols and objects that are remembered vividly by those who lived through it. Many members of the older generation were shocked and outraged by the "Roaring Twenties" with its "flaming youth" who defied established customs. The ensuing clash of values was a part of the dynamism of the era.

Some of the things that characterized the decade were: Prohibition, bootleg whiskey, gang wars, revivalistic preaching, materialism, speculation in real estate and stock, automobiles, roadhouses and speakeasies, anti-evolutionism, cigarette smoking, short hair and short skirts for women, the second Ku Klux Klan, jazz and ragtime music, and the Charleston and other wild dances. With the possible exception of gang wars, all of these were a part of the Twenties in Memphis. They were mainly matters of social and cultural change that offended editorial writers and preachers, but had limited effect on the economic and political life of the city.

Like other Americans, Memphians had lived through World War I and the idealism of Woodrow Wilson's great crusade to make the world safe for democracy. If they were tired of Wilson's progressive New Freedom, they were still proud of the war and their city's enthusiastic part in it. They agreed with the desire of their new president, Warren G. Harding, to return to "normalcy." They were ready to enjoy life and to make money.

Memphis remained generally prosperous, which meant that the bank did also, until the end of the decade. The decline of cotton continued, mostly because of overproduction and reduced prices. Nothing could be done to reverse the trend. The Bluff City was still dangerously dependent on cotton and lumber, but some industries did well. The value of industrial products increased to $91.7 million in 1927.

By this year, the Bank of Commerce and Trust Company had become the largest and most successful financial institution in Memphis. According to information provided by the library of the Federal Reserve Bank of St. Louis, the Bank of Commerce and Trust Company had total resources of $37.6 million, while Union and Planters Bank and Trust Company was listed with resources of $35.6 million, and First National Bank reported a total of $21.8 million. In the total of deposits, the Bank of Commerce and Trust Company also led with $32.1 million, while Union and Planters had $31.6 million, and First National had only $19.5 million. The Bank of Commerce and Trust Company had the largest amount of listed capital at $3 million, followed by Union and Planters with $2.5 million, and First National with $1 million. The Bank of Commerce and Trust Company also had the largest listed surplus, of $1.5 million, followed by First National with $800,000, and Union and Planters with a surplus and undivided profit of $728,000. It seems certain that the Bank of Commerce and Trust Company was the largest financial institution in Tennessee at this time. All Nashville banks listed smaller amounts of resources and capitalization. They also held smaller amounts of deposits. The largest deposit totals were: American National Bank, $21,997,000; Fourth and First National Bank, $20,318,000; Nashville Trust Company, $9,929,000 (which also listed trust deposits of $14,389,000); and Commerce Union Bank, $7,164,000.

Still the hardwood flooring capital of the nation, Memphis was producing 300 million feet of hardwood lumber, as well as other wood products, annually. The cottonseed products industry increased through the decade. The Fisher Body Company, the American Car and Foundry Company, and the Ford Motor Company assembly plant all contributed to the economy of the city.

The prosperity of the decade made it one of the active times in Memphis history for the construction of major commercial and institutional buildings. Some of those completed by the first half of the 1920s were the Peabody Hotel, the Cotton Exchange Building, Lowenstein's Department Store, the William Len Hotel, the Farnsworth Building, Ellis Auditorium, the Methodist Hospital, and the Sears and Roebuck Building.

Some institutional buildings were in use at the beginning of the decade. They included Brooks Memorial Art Gallery, St. Joseph Hospital, Baptist Hospital, LeMoyne Institute, the University of Tennessee Medical School, State Teachers College, and Southwestern (now Rhodes College), which was moving to Memphis from Clarksville. The Orpheum occupied two structures during the decade. One build-

ing stood until 1923 when it burned during an unexpectedly exciting performance, and the new Orpheum was completed in 1928. Another structure, Cla-Le-Claire, was built as the residence of grocery magnate Clarence Saunders, but was lost to him when he declared bankruptcy in 1924. It has since become the Pink Palace Museum.

The Bank of Commerce and Trust Company passed two significant milestones in its history during the decade; the first of these was reached in 1923, the second in 1929. The first, announced on January 9, 1923, was the merger with the Commercial Trust and Savings Bank. By this time, the Bank of Commerce and Trust Company's total deposits had reached $40 million, and the Commercial Trust and Savings Bank had deposits of approximately $7.5 million. After absorbing its smaller neighboring institution, the Bank of Commerce and Trust Company had total resources of about $40 million. This made it the largest bank in its area and one of the largest in the South.

Founded in 1905, the Commercial Trust and Savings Bank had operated successfully, but had not grown to a size competitive with the larger banks of the city. It carried some major accounts and its operations were profitable enough that its stock was merged share for share with that of the Bank of Commerce and Trust Company. The death of its strong executive officer, Dwight Armstrong, in December 1922, had caused its president, Abe Goodman, and its directors to seek the merger. Its building at the northeast corner of Main Street and Union Avenue, as well as another adjacent building occupied by a Piggly Wiggly store, became the property of the Bank of Commerce and Trust Company. Abe Goodman was added to the Board of Directors and his employees simply moved their place of work the short distance to the bank they had joined.

This acquisition brought a substantial increase in the volume of business transacted by the Bank of Commerce and Trust Company. There was also a great increase in the lending opportunities available to banks throughout the nation during the 1920s. The

In the late 1920s, the Bank of Commerce and Trust Company would design and construct its own building — one that would be planned from the beginning to meet the needs of its operations. Pictured here is an architectural rendering, by Hanker and Cairns Architects, of the new building at the southwest corner of Monroe Avenue and Second Street.

decade brought one of the greatest booms of speculative financing in the financial history of the nation. A virtual mania of speculation seemed to sweep across the United States. Many banks became perilously overextended during this era, but the Bank of Commerce and Trust Company seems to have fared better than most financial institutions because of its traditionally conservative leadership and its custom of generally limiting loans to local customers whose credit standing was well known.

In 1927, however, the directors of the bank had the sad duty of memorializing the death of one of their members and former president, Oliver Hazard Perry Piper. His death at the age of 89 at his winter home in Florida brought to a close an era in the history of the bank. He was the last of the group of men who had met in 1873 to organize the bank in its first home at 12 Madison Street in Memphis. The old veteran Confederate artilleryman was buried in Elmwood Cemetery where so many of his former comrades in arms had been laid to rest. He had served his bank for more than half of a century.

By the time of Piper's death, the Bank of Commerce and Trust Company had begun to take action that would lead to one of the major changes in its operation. During the prosperous boom decade of the 1920s, Thomas Vinton continued to serve as president, although he relied heavily on the counsel of R. Brinkley Snowden who remained as vice president. Apparently no important decisions were ever made without Snowden's approval. The problem the bank experienced was a direct result of the unprecedented growth of its business. The bank had simply grown to the extent that the building on Main Street no longer contained enough space for its needs.

Accordingly, the decision had to be made to relocate the bank in a structure large enough to handle its still expanding activities. This time, however, the bank would design and construct its own building — one that would be planned from the beginning to meet the needs of its operations and to serve as a fitting symbol of the solidity and wealth of the preeminent bank of the Mid-South. Many new commercial and institutional buildings, most of which still stand, were being erect-

A total of $2 million, an unusually large amount for the time, was budgeted for the new Bank of Commerce and Trust Company building, pictured here circa 1935.

ed throughout the city during this prosperous decade, but the one planned by the bank would surpass them all in grandeur. Land was acquired for it, consisting of a full quarter of a block at the southwest corner of Second Street and Monroe Avenue. Capital was available, for the institution's profits were substantial and it had continued its custom of keeping a large amount of money designated as surplus. A total of $2 million, an unusually large amount for the time, was budgeted for the building and the architectural firm of Hanker and Cairns was commissioned to prepare the plans, although it may certainly be assumed that the officers and directors of the bank directed the form the design would follow.

It is apparent that the amount of capital they committed to its construction was matched by the thoroughness of their search for a model for this first building created specifically for their use. They found it in the Mellon Bank in Pittsburgh, long believed to be

one of the most imposing financial institutions in America. The architectural plans for the Mellon building were acquired from the firm of McKim, Mead and White by Hanker and Cairns and adapted moderately to suit the needs of the Memphis bank. Some observers have considered the new design to be an improvement on the original one.

If the architects intended to construct an edifice that would stand the test of time, they were successful. Turning back to the influence of classic Grecian architecture, they designed a building so perfect in proportion that photographs cannot convey an accurate sense of its massive size. It is necessary to stand outside its walls or stand in its lobby to gain a true perspective of its dimensions. Eugene Johnson and Robert Russell's *Architectural Guide* states: "The proportions are based on the Golden Section favored by the ancient Greeks, or at least on a three-by-five plan that comes close to the Golden Section in proportion. (The ratio of the

Opened in November 1929, the bank's new lobby was dominated by 22 columns of Bottichino marble, each 32 feet in height. A 660 square-foot skylight gave light to the interior. Containing what was reported to be the first air conditioning system in Memphis, the building was as modern as technology of the time could make it.

Golden Section is 1 to 1.618.)" The classic Doric influence is revealed in the exterior with its tall, fluted columns and heavy bronze doors and grille work. From their base of polished Stone Mountain granite, the walls of fine-textured Indiana limestone rose skyward.

Ancient Greek architecture at its best was demonstrated in the interior, following the Ionic form. Twenty-two columns of Bottichino marble, each 32 feet in height, extended upward to support the high ceiling. A skylight, of 660 square feet, gave light to the interior, aided by large windows on all sides. Marble was used almost entirely throughout the spacious lobby, with entrances between both exterior and interior columns from Monroe Avenue and Second Street.

The building was as modern as technology of the time could make it. It contained what was reported to be the first air conditioning system in Memphis. The basement, entered from the door on Second

Street, contained the ornate directors' room, 5,000 safety deposit boxes and the huge steel money vault designed by Hanker and Cairns. It was entered by a massive, round steel door that weighed 26 tons but was balanced as lightly as a feather.

Today, after some renovations and a few minor changes, the building still stands, looking as impressive now as it must have in 1929. Currently serving as the headquarters and main office of the bank, it still has no rival in classical architecture in the city. Indeed, if there is any other bank structure in the South comparable to this building, it is unknown to the officers now serving. It was entered onto the National Register of Historic Places of the United States Department of the Interior on May 7, 1980.

Moving the largest financial institution of the area from one building to another was a major undertaking. The move was scheduled for November 11, 1929, which date was probably wisely selected, because Armistice Day (now Veterans Day) was an important state and national holiday. In a meticulously planned movement, a caravan under armed guard quickly moved $23 million in cash and securities from the old vault on Main Street to the one in the new building. The Bank of Commerce and Trust Company thus moved to the location that would be its home to the present.

There is no doubt that the construction of the new building met a critical need of the bank and provided it with a physical asset of great value; however, the timing of its opening was not favorable. The fall of 1929 marked the end of the Roaring Twenties with its orgy of speculation and rapid business growth, and began a completely different era, the Depression Decade. The national economy reached the watershed of change on "Black Thursday," October 24, the day prices took a record fall on the New York Stock Exchange. About $5 billion of stock value disappeared that day, but worse was yet to come.

On October 29, 13 days before the opening of the bank's new building, in a disaster that spread throughout the nation, the stock market collapsed. The wealth built up through the decade of prosperity was gone. When the news reached Memphis, it must have caused some of the bank's officers and directors to wonder if they might not have a serious need for the $2 million they had spent for their new building. In the newspapers of the city, however, the stock market crash

Within a year after the stock market crash, the Depression began to spread across the city like a 19th century plague, bringing hardship on a scale never before experienced. The adversities of the Depression were compounded by the Memphis flood of 1937. Pictured here are flood victims in the Fairgrounds Refugee Camp mess hall.

received surprisingly little notice. To citizens of a provincial Southern city dependent on a single crop that grew with the regularity of the seasons, New York seemed far away.

Memphians did not understand how interconnected, nor how fragile, the national economy had become. Besides, they were assured by President Herbert Hoover, their newspapers, and the local business leaders that there was no danger to their city. In the beginning, these authorities were right. Cotton crops were planted as usual, banks in the city remained open, and few residents had the kind of industrial jobs that would be among the first affected by the collapse of the nation's prime capital market. In fact, for Memphis boosters, 1930 brought good news. The U. S. census reported that Memphis was now a city of more than a quarter of a million inhabitants, the official count being 253,143. City officials, obsessed with the importance of growth, had done their best to achieve it, annexing 20.3 square miles of suburban land to boost the population.

Disaster was slow in coming to the city, but it arrived nonetheless. Within a year after the stock market crash, the Depression began to spread across the city like a 19th century plague, bringing hardship on a scale never before experienced. About a third of Memphis' manufacturing business disappeared. The closing of the Fisher Body Company put 1,200 men out of work. Ford Motor Company remained open, but it had to fire some employees and had work only part of each year for the rest.

Purchasing power decreased, and those who had money were afraid to spend it. By 1933, retail sales had declined more than 50 percent, almost one out of four stores had failed, causing the loss of even more jobs. Banks foreclosed on businesses large and small, and leading businessmen found themselves unable to pay their debts. Some major Memphis institutions failed, among them the Porter Building, the Shrine Building, the Sterick Building, and the Parkview Hotel. Citizens stopped paying their taxes and it became impossible for property owners to collect rents. They could evict their renters, and sometimes did, but there were no others with money to replace them.

The depression also spread through American agriculture, and cotton prices fell sharply. In 1933, the price of cotton was at 5 cents a pound, less than the cost of growing it, and the distribution network through which it passed from planter to manufacturer was clogged with a three-year supply of unsold cotton. This, of course, had been a principal area of investment by the bank.

Despite the widespread failure of financial institutions throughout the nation during the first years of the Depression, Memphis banks passed through the hard times with fewer problems than usual, perhaps because of their traditionally conservative management and the relatively isolated area of their activities. But the era did bring difficulties. Two words that had always been feared by bankers were "embezzlement" and "run." The Bank of Commerce and Trust Company experienced, and survived, both of these during the early depression period.

Fortunately, the bank has suffered very few instances of dishonesty by its officers during its long history, but the first of these — or at least the first to come to public attention — was exposed in August 1932. A vice president who had transferred to service in the institution when it acquired the Commercial Trust and Savings Bank in 1923 had found himself in person-

al financial difficulties as a result of the stock market crash. He was arrested on charges of forgery and fraudulent breach of trust involving about $100,000 from the bank. T. O. Vinton and R. Brinkley Snowden quickly assured the public through newspaper notices that the offending official was no longer associated with the bank and that the losses were more than covered by the surety bond of $300,000 required for vice presidents so that the institution would incur no loss from the incident.

Less than five months later, the Bank of Commerce and Trust Company had its first experience with the other most dreaded occurrence among bankers — a run. Such an event is a mass action when all or a substantial part of the depositors simultaneously rush (some, of course, actually run) to their bank in order to withdraw their money. Such runs are caused by a fear, either realistic or unfounded, that the institution is failing; hence, their necessity to recover their funds quickly before the collapse takes place. An irony is that such runs have frequently caused financial institutions to fail, even if there were no actual danger of it happening if the run had not started.

Runs had taken place throughout the financial history of the city, and numerous banks had been forced out of business as a result of them. Bankers virtually never kept enough cash on hand to allow all deposits to be withdrawn at the same time. Banking had thus always been based to a large degree on trust, hence the imperative need for banks to maintain the appearance of stability and prosperity. When this necessary trust was overcome by fear for the safety of their money, the mass panic of depositors caused their run on the bank. Union Planters Bank had experienced a run, caused by completely unfounded rumors, in 1928.

The run on the Bank of Commerce and Trust Company came in January 1933. Its statement of December 31, 1932, had listed a substantial deposit total of $21,250,000, but rumors of trouble spread through the city during the next two weeks, and depositors began withdrawing their money. The amount of deposits fell to about $18 million, and, although the movement had not yet reached the proportions of a run, the situation was so dangerous that if something could not be done quickly the bank would be lost. On Thursday, January 19, the officers and directors were called into an all-day meeting and a critical week in the history of the bank began.

It was fortunate for the bank that the next day, Friday, January 20, was Robert E. Lee's birthday, a state holiday which allowed the bank to remain closed. Full-page newspaper notices headed "To The Public" were published by the bank that day, assuring readers that the institution was solvent and would meet all its obligations. They were signed by the officers: T. O. Vinton, president; S. J. Shepherd, vice president and counsel; R. Brinkley Snowden, vice president; L. A. Thornton, vice president; R. B. Barton, vice president; and A. C. Burchett, vice president and cashier. Gilmer Winston, president of Union Planters National Bank and Trust Company, and S. E. Ragland, president of First National Bank, added their endorsement that the Bank of Commerce and Trust Company was amply able to take care of its depositors.

This notice may have helped, but it did not stem the tide of fear that was spreading through the city. Since the next day was Saturday, the bank was able to

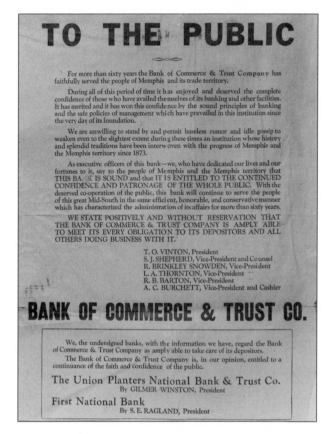

January 20, 1933, this full-page notice, which ran in The Commercial Appeal *with the headline "To the Public," affirmed that the bank was amply able to meet its obligations. An editorial by the newspaper in the same edition congratulated the bank for the frank and open manner in which it reassured the public of its soundness, and condemned the "careless talking" that made such an assurance necessary.*

close at noon, but the withdrawals continued during the hours it was open. Sunday was doubtless a day of apprehension for the officers and directors of the bank. This concern was justified. During the day they opened negotiations toward the possible merger with one of the other major banks in the city, but they also began receiving encouraging reports from Washington concerning an application they had made on Thursday to the Reconstruction Finance Corporation for an emergency loan of $10 million. Officials of the RFC and the Federal Reserve System in Memphis remained in contact with the bank throughout the day. Strong congressional support was being given by Senator Kenneth McKellar and Congressman Edward H. Crump.

The bank needed all the assistance it could get, because on Monday, January 23, the much dreaded run developed. Crowds gathered in the streets around the bank and according to newspaper accounts "Lines of depositors surged against the tellers' cages." The Memphis Police Department arrived to keep order and officers and friends of the bank passed among the crowd, urging customers to keep their deposits in the institution, but the fears continued and so did the withdrawals.

By the close of the day, deposits had dropped to about $16 million and the situation was grave. The bank had only about $3 million in cash, and there was no indication that the run was abating. The RFC loan of $10 million had been approved, but in order to meet all obligations another $3 million had to be secured. There was no thought of giving up by anyone involved.

Directors, officers, and friends of the bank gathered in the directors' room downstairs and began a long and crucial night of feverish activity under great pressure. Their efforts involved activity both in Washington and Memphis. Telephone contact was maintained through the night with RFC officials in Washington. The bank immediately asked the RFC for an additional loan of $3 million, but this request was refused unless the bank could raise an additional $2.5 million on its own. Work began immediately and continued through the night to secure the necessary funds. Lists of major depositors were given to various friends of the bank who drove through the city during the night to persuade them to sign an agreement pledging to freeze their accounts and make no withdrawals during the period of crisis. Sixty years later, in 1993, attorney Benjamin Goodman still has vivid memories of driving through the Memphis night to secure signatures to these agreements from depositors he knew. All of those on whom he called signed the papers.

There was also activity and no sleep through the night at the Federal Reserve branch in Memphis where W. R. King, Wilson Mallory, Phil Canale, and Paul Dillard maintained their own telephone connections with the RFC in Washington. During the hours

Alonzo Locke

between midnight and dawn, the battle was won. Officers and friends began returning with their pledges and the money was raised. The RFC telephoned approval of its additional $3 million loan and the bank was saved.

Withdrawals continued through Tuesday, January 24, and began to decrease by Wednesday, January 25. Speeches urging confidence in the bank were made to those in the waiting lines by Mayor Watkins Overton; Ed McCadden, attorney; Walter Armstrong, speaking for Memphis Power and Light Company; R. L. Jones, superintendent of the city schools; and many others. Bank officers now recollect the work of Alonzo Locke, long associated with the Peabody Hotel, who came to speak to black depositors waiting in lines outside the bank.

The Bank of Commerce and Trust Company was saved by its friends. During its years of faithful and efficient service, it had won the trust and friendship of many of its customers and associates. Without their support, it would not have survived this crisis. A complete list of those who came to its aid is too extensive to include in this text, but some are easily identified today. Seven members of the Snowden family combined their assistance to provide more than $100,000 in cash and collateral. Members of the Canale family joined together to make a substantial contribution — as did W. B. Mallory and Company, R. B. Barton, and J. Goldsmith and Sons Company. Abe Plough put up $50,000 and more than doubled the amount two days later; the American Snuff Company pledged $50,000; William R. Moore,

The Bank of Commerce and Trust Company applied for and received its second national charter, becoming National Bank of Commerce on May 1, 1933. This 1940 photograph pictures the building bearing the bank's new name.

$50,000; R. R. Prest, $57,000; and Hugh Fulghum, Memphis manager of Kroger Grocery and Baking Company, $70,000. Union Planters National Bank and Trust Company added $250,000, and S. E. Ragland, president of First National Bank, in a public gesture of support, reportedly sent carts loaded with money down the street from his bank. Many other prominent people in the city also added their pledges to the total.

By Wednesday, January 25, the crisis was clearly over. An armored motor truck from the Federal Reserve Bank brought the first shipment of $1 million to be placed in the vault for the payment of depositors. A photograph in the *Memphis Press-Scimitar* showed armed guards carrying sacks of money into the bank past the large crowd still waiting outside. A sign, painted in red and black letters, was placed at the Monroe Avenue entrance to the building.

The sign read: "The Bank of Commerce & Trust Co. has enough money on hand to pay every depositor and will remain open all day and night, if necessary, to pay all depositors who wish to withdraw their money." It was not necessary, though, for the bank to remain open late. By mid-afternoon, the people waiting in lines had gone home and there was not a single customer in the lobby to make a withdrawal. The run was over.

Those who had worked through that long and difficult Monday night to save the bank always remembered their shared pleasure of accomplishment and much appreciated feast of beer and sandwiches which the bank served to them in the directors' room in the hours before dawn when their work was completed. So long as the bank officers of the time lived, they always had a special appreciation and affection for the many friends and customers, large and small, who made their contributions toward the saving of the bank.

One lesson learned from this time of trouble was the necessity of governmental support. Accordingly, the Bank of Commerce and Trust Company applied for and received its second national charter. On May 1,

1933, it became the National Bank of Commerce in Memphis. It also acquired new leadership. Thomas O. Vinton retired from the presidency and was replaced by William R. King, a director who had been associated with the bank since 1920. At the time he assumed the bank presidency he was serving as president of the William R. Moore Dry Goods Company, Memphis' oldest and largest wholesale firm of its kind. During the remainder of the decade, while he served as president, the bank again returned to growth and prosperity. By 1940, its deposits had increased 300 percent.

By this date National Bank of Commerce had more than recovered from the difficulties of its run and the Depression. The new decade was marked by an occasion, even though it was not a happy one, that brought the Memphis banking community together. It was the funeral at Calvary Episcopal Church of Thomas O. Vinton, former president of the Bank of Commerce and Trust Company.

The list of active and honorary pallbearers is illustrative because it is a roster of Memphis banking leaders of the time. It included: R. Brinkley Snowden, J. Bayard Snowden, Vance Alexander, I. H. Wilson, S. E. Ragland, R. L. Taylor, Joe Montedonico, Sr., Whitfield King, John Fox, John Phillips, Col. Walter Canada, J. Seddon Allen, Judge Sam O. Bates, Martin Dunscomb, H. Price Curd, Lawrence S. Gwyn, Wick Ransom, James L. Ross, Shepherd Tate, M. E. Carter, Bethell Edrington, Leslie Thornton, Abe Plough, Cleland K. Smith, Hubert K. Reese, McKay Van Vleet, William G. Phillips, James H. Fisher, Richard H. Anderson, Brown Burch, H. E. Buckingham, Neely Grant, Phil Pidgeon, R. B. Snowden, Jr., Swayne Latham, John Phillips, Jr., D. O. Andrews, and Sidney Farnsworth. The names in this assembly included both those who had led the financial community of Memphis during generations past and those who would continue to lead it during forthcoming decades.

The Second Street entrance to the National Bank of Commerce building.

CHAPTER SIX

PROGRESS THROUGH THE 20TH CENTURY: BANKING DURING QUIET TIMES

After receiving its second charter from the federal government, National Bank of Commerce passed through two successive memorable decades, each characterized indelibly by the influence of a single historical event of such force that it shaped the course of the nation and all its institutions. Just as the Thirties had been dominated by and identified with the Great Depression, the Forties were formed by the influence of World War II. In economic terms, these two dominant events were as opposite as night and day. The Great Depression brought the American economy to a standstill, while World War II forced it to the maximum limits of productivity and expansion.

Although the times and the national economy changed as the decade of the Thirties ended and the Forties began, National Bank of Commerce maintained a remarkable continuity of leadership. For the bank, the decade began on January 9, 1940, with an event that might have seemed to outside observers to indicate a major change for the institution. William Rufus King retired from the position of president and the directors replaced him with another chief executive officer, Richard Bethel Barton. Actually, there was no noticeable alteration in the policy and operations of the bank. Both King and Barton had served the bank since the 1920s, and both continued to serve it for the remainder of their lives. The only change in 1940 was in their titles. Barton moved from executive vice president to president, and King went from president to chairman of the Board of Directors.

The history of National Bank of Commerce has always been influenced by the personality of its chief executives, but some have had a stronger and longer lasting effect than others. In the constellation of strong individuals who have led the bank, William King occupies a prominent position. His service to the bank extended over a period of 43 years. He had been a

director for 13 years before being elected as president. After retiring from the position of president, he served over a decade as chairman of the Board of Directors, after which he served for more than another decade as honorary chairman of the board. His direct influence over the bank lasted until the mid-1960s.

Born in Hempstead County, Arkansas, five years after the Bank of Commerce was founded, he grew up in Texarkana, Arkansas, where he attended public schools. Like most of the other early presidents of the bank, he was essentially a self-made man. His only higher education seems to have been a business college course, but he did much private reading and study. He also read law while serving as a stenographer for an attorney in Guntersville, Alabama. Arriving in Memphis in 1898, he took a position as stenographer and bookkeeper for the William R. Moore Dry Goods Company. His dedication and ability won successive promotions to assistant credit manager, credit manager, secretary-treasurer, vice president and general manager, and in 1932, president. This last position he held until 1958.

Described as "probably the most widely known merchant in the Mid-South," he continued the tradition of mercantile influence in the management of National Bank of Commerce. Although without training or experience in banking, "he brought his exceptional merchandising ability and his wide personal acquaintance with business men throughout the Mid-South." Actively involved in the life of the community, he served as a director of the Illinois Central Railroad, the Memphis branch of the Federal Reserve Bank of St. Louis, and the Commerce Title Guaranty Company. This latter firm had previously been a department of the bank and still worked closely with its former parent institution.

Well liked by all who knew him, he served as president and treasurer of the board of trustees of the William R. Moore School of Technology, a charter member of the Memphis Rotary Club, and a member of the First Presbyterian Church of Memphis. When his duties to the William R. Moore Company caused him finally to retire as active chairman of the Board of Directors of the bank, the members elevated him to honorary chairman and cited his service as follows: "...he is like the sturdy oak which grapples with the blasts of many storms and, when they eventually subside, stands stronger in its position by reason of the struggle...We admire him, respect him, and hold him dear in a way which defies any wordy description."

His photograph, with strong cheekbones and deep-set, piercing eyes, reveals a man of stern and uncompromising character, whose appearance must

William Rufus King

have inspired confidence among depositors that their money would be absolutely safe in his control. He and the other officers who had been with the bank during the run and the near loss of the institution that followed it were understandably influenced by the need for safety and caution in all financial operations. This was a wise course during the troubled years of the depression. The bank survived and operated successfully and profitably.

Although William King remained as chairman of the Board of Directors, Richard Bethel Barton, who assumed the presidency of the bank in 1940, made a major contribution of his own to the institution. His main interest was cotton, and he renewed the long established tradition of the bank as a leading supporter of this industry. During his term as president, Memphis kept its position as the world's largest spot cotton market, and his institution became the world's largest cotton bank. (A spot market is one in which the commodity is bought and sold on the spot, in contrast to a futures market.)

Born on June 1, 1881, at the Barton Brothers Plantation near Mound City, Arkansas, he grew up surrounded by cotton. He was educated by private tutors until the age of 15, and then attended the University of Arkansas where he received a degree in law in 1902. After living in his native state for several years, he moved to Memphis in 1907 to enter the cotton business. He soon became one of the most popular and successful men in the entire cotton district on Front Street. By 1924, he had advanced to the presidency of the F.G. Barton Cotton Company, later to be followed by service as chairman of its board of directors.

A strong supporter of the public life of his city, he was elected in 1926 as president of the Memphis Cotton Exchange. He also joined the elite group of community leaders who served as members of the Memphis Park Commission, a position he held for 10 years, devoting special effort toward providing outdoor recreational facilities for young people. Having become acquainted with William King, whose views he shared, he agreed to accept a position as vice president of the Bank of Commerce and Trust Company in 1927. He labored loyally with King through the great financial crisis of 1933, and continued to serve with him as his executive vice president after the reorganization as National Bank of Commerce.

After assuming the presidency of the bank in 1940, he continued to serve King and the other directors with his organizational talent and his detailed knowledge of the major economic activity of the area. Robert Talley paid the following tribute to his contribution: "'Dick' Barton knew cotton every inch of the way from seed to finished textiles. It was by reason of his thorough and complete knowledge of cotton production and cotton marketing that the National Bank of Commerce came to operate the largest collateral department in the world for the handling of cotton doc-

Richard Bethel Barton

uments, both as its own collateral and as custodian for the collateral of others."

Such a major area of operations of the bank was well understood at the time, but probably deserves some explanation now. After the annual cotton crop throughout the entire region was ginned, baled, and loaded into railroad cars or warehouses, all of the millions of bales were designated by bills of lading or warehouse receipts. These papers were known as cotton documents.

The large cotton shippers required considerable amounts of capital in order to assemble substantial consignments of bales for shipment to the mills. These cotton documents were pledged to their banks for loans they had to secure. The total amount of capital available in Memphis was not nearly enough to supply the needs of the region's cotton crop, so the large shippers had to borrow money from other financial centers throughout the world and pledge their cotton documents as collateral. Since each time a bale of cotton was removed from a warehouse the cotton document had to be surrendered, it was not feasible to actually send these documents to all the banks that provided funds. Therefore, in order to keep their documents in a single, accessible place, the shippers developed the practice of depositing the documents with National Bank of Commerce in Memphis as custodian for the other lending banks.

This preeminent position in the industry held by National Bank of Commerce could not have been achieved without the trust and respect of financial leaders throughout the world. The bank came to be the custodian of cotton documents for more than 70 other banks from California to London, including 14 of the 20 largest banks in the United States, as well as for many other institutions that financed cotton. Bank officers eventually estimated that their collateral department handled more than 2.5 million bales annually in these exchanges.

Banking operations, like all other activities in the city of Memphis during this era, were carried on under the influence of wartime. Like the crash of the New York stock market in 1929 that foretold the Great Depression, an event had taken place in Europe in 1939 that heralded a new era for the United States. Within two years, it would bring a tidal wave of change to Memphis. Adolf Hitler, the dictator of Nazi Germany, had launched a war that threatened to spread beyond Europe.

American political leaders, including Franklin Roosevelt, foresaw their nation's involvement in this conflict. And at some point, possibly as early as 1940, Memphis business and political leaders became aware of the approach of war. Whenever the war might arrive, there were three predictable certainties about it. The first was that the citizens of Memphis would give complete support to the nation's entry into the war. True to the tradition of the Volunteer State of which they were a part, they had supported every war their country had fought since the city was founded.

The second certainty was that the federal government would spend great quantities of money and the entire national economy would undergo inflation as a result of it. Twentieth century war had become increasingly expensive, and it was obvious that this conflict would be a major one.

The third predictable fact was that a substantial part of federal wartime spending would be done in the Bluff City. Political boss Edward H. Crump and U.S. Senator Kenneth McKellar, both Memphians, were among the president's strongest partisans in the South. They had already proven their influence with Roosevelt by securing maximum federal spending for Memphis.

Memphis' economic condition had improved by 1940, despite some lingering effects of the Depression. Its population had grown to 292,942 even though the city government, hard pressed to handle the space it included, had not annexed any new territory during the Thirties.

Most of the news for Memphis was favorable during the year. National spending did indeed arrive. The Chickasaw Ordnance Works plant, costing $25 million and operated by E. I. duPont de Nemours, began producing military explosives at a site north of the city. The Second Army Headquarters, with its payroll and purchasing needs, was moved from Chicago to Memphis. Chicago and Southern Airlines announced the movement of its headquarters to the city, and 20 new industries, although some of them were small, began operations.

The next year brought more progress for the city, and the arrival of the war. Defense spending continued with the beginning of a $17 million U.S. Quartermaster Depot on Airways. Unlike many of the wartime projects, it has remained in Memphis to the present. Other construction during the year included a large munitions plant near Cordova by the National Fireworks Company.

On December 7, 1941, a date still remembered vividly by many Memphians living at the time, Japanese warplanes attacked the U.S. Navy at Pearl Harbor. The nation officially entered the war against Japan, Germany, and Italy. World War II had begun, and Memphis was ready.

Local citizens were so eager to enter the war that the recruiting station in the post office building had to be operated 24 hours a day to handle the crowd. About 160,000 Shelby County residents registered for service and approximately 40,000 were inducted for active duty, including a number of officers and employees of National Bank of Commerce.

The War Department predictably increased its spending in Memphis after the war began. The Fourth Ferrying Group Command Base was placed in the city, and headquartered at the airport, which necessarily had to be expanded. This move brought an expenditure of $3 million for improvement that remained after the war ended. An Air Force Depot was built on Jackson Avenue and extensive U.S. Navy facilities were constructed at the old Park Field site near Millington. These included a Naval Air Technical Training Center, a Naval Hospital, and a Naval Air Station. All of the installations involved large expenditures for payrolls, materials, and supplies.

Major industrial firms moved to the city or expanded plants to engage in war production. Some of the larger ones were Plough Inc., Ford Motor Company, Firestone, Continental Can Company, Quaker Oats, Fisher Aircraft Division of General Motors, and Kimberly-Clark. Memphis had at last acquired a substantial base of manufacturing, even though it might be temporary. Because they were all engaged in military production funded by the federal government, the long-term status of these plants in the city was doubtful.

But some of the projects brought in during this era became permanent assets of the city. The most important of the military installations was Kennedy General Hospital. Construction began in 1942 at an initial cost of $10 million. Designed to have 1,500 beds, it was built on a 129-acre cotton field at Park and Shotwell bought by Memphis and Shelby County for the War Department. This latter street name was changed to Getwell after it was noted that men wounded in battle might not like being hospitalized beside a street of that name. By the end of the war, 44,000 wounded and ill soldiers had been treated at Kennedy. In 1946, the hospital became part of the Veterans Administration, and during the Sixties it was moved to a new building near the medical center of the University of Tennessee.

The war came to an end in August 1945, after the surrender of Japan. The Shelby County servicemen, except for the 662 who had died in the war, began returning to their homes. Most of the wartime industries were closed during the next few months, but the accumulated capital of the era and the great demand for civilian goods — delayed during the four years of hostilities — continued the growth and economic expansion through the remainder of the decade.

Financial information published at the beginning of this era indicated that all three national banks of the city had survived the Depression times in sound condition, and had benefitted from the general economic recovery brought by the policies of the New Deal. Although National Bank of Commerce had increased in size and had operated profitably, it had lost its pre-eminent position in relation to the other leading banks in Memphis. In 1940, its assets and liabilities had reached a level of $34,408,852.26, and it had a deposit total of $31,036,753.38. But at this time First National Bank's assets and liabilities had increased to $58,297,120.28, and it held total deposits of $54,162,986.72. Union Planters National Bank had reached a total of assets and liabilities of $86,916,668.08, and had total deposits of $77,419,099.05. It was thus the largest bank in the city, and National Bank of Commerce had declined to third from first place.

All Memphis financial institutions grew and prospered through the remainder of the decade, mainly because of the general prosperity brought by greatly increased governmental spending. The extensive construction and operation of military installations and civilian plants for wartime manufacturing brought a large amount of money into the city. Strict national regulation of wages, prices, and rents, as well as rationing of most goods available for civilian consumption, served to limit the inflation that took place as a result of the increased spending. These generally successful efforts to stabilize the value of the currency were helpful to creditor institutions, including banks.

The three major banks of the city gained during this era. National Bank of Commerce strengthened its dominant position with the cotton industry, which enjoyed a boom during the decade; but Union Planters National Bank benefited from a different influence. According to Robert G. Snowden, who has clear recollections of the era, Edward H. Crump, "was such a strong individual and controlled so much of the economy...was very strong for the Union Planters Bank and he promoted Union Planters." At no other time in the history of the city has any single person exercised so much control over the politics and the economy as Mr. Crump did during these years that are identified by his name, "The Crump Era." With the support of his highly organized political machine, the entire Shelby County legislative delegation, and U. S. Senator Kenneth McKellar, Crump made certain that public funds in Memphis — federal, state, and local — were

Edward Hull Crump

spent as he desired. There is no way to measure the quantitative value of this support to his favorite bank, but there is no doubt that it was substantial.

By the close of the decade, in 1949, National Bank of Commerce had grown noticeably, having more than doubled its assets. But it had fallen even further behind its two major competitors, each of which had approximately tripled in size. Union Planters National Bank listed $244,122,442.56 in assets and $227,973,604.97 in deposits, First National Bank reported $174,563,348.32 in assets and $164,943,762.43 in deposits, but National Bank of Commerce had

assets of only $78,978,111.81 and deposits totaling $73,795,059.27. While it had operated profitably, it had dropped further behind the other leading banks, both in actual growth and in the percentage of increase. A state chartered institution, the Commercial and Industrial Bank, was also in operation, in the Sterick Building; but it held assets of only $10,429,476.20 and deposits of $8,753,147.89.

During the Forties, therefore, the operations of National Bank of Commerce were characterized by a great deal of stability and only limited change. Much of the growth the bank did achieve was a result of its increasing role of service to the cotton business. According to an article in *The Commercial Appeal* in August 1944, the average cotton crop in the United States for the previous three years had been 11,353,624 bales. This bank alone during that period had handled 7,018,570 bales, an average of 2,339,523 bales per year, or 21 percent of the entire cotton crop of the nation. Bank officers estimated that their cotton department handled more than 5 million documents each year in exchange.

Two events of significance took place at the bank during 1947. One was the installation in May of 12 Burroughs commercial teller's machines at the counters in the bank. Reported to save about 30 percent of the time involved in each checking account deposit transaction, these machines enabled tellers to quickly

The installation in May 1947 of 12 Burroughs commercial teller's machines reportedly saved about 30 percent of the time involved in each checking account deposit transaction. Individual and industrial depositors no longer needed to carry their passbooks to the bank to have their accounts balanced by hand.

enter the account number and deposit total and give each customer a printed receipt. It was no longer necessary for individual and industrial depositors to carry their passbooks to the bank to have their accounts balanced by hand. Account balances were then mailed out in monthly statements.

The other major event of the year 1947 was the completion of the final phase of the liquidation of the old Bank of Commerce and Trust Company which had begun when National Bank of Commerce was rechartered in 1933. At this time the charter of the old bank was surrendered and all of its stockholders had received shares of the stock of the new bank. National Bank of Commerce stockholders received the shares of the Commerce Title Guaranty Company which owned and continued to operate in the old bank building at 14-18 South Main Street. A.L. Pritchard, who had directed the liquidation since 1933, continued to serve

as president of Commerce Title Guaranty Company and was also made vice chairman of the Board of Directors of National Bank of Commerce.

During the following year, the directors had to deal again with the succession of leadership for the bank. Richard B. Barton, who had served as president for eight years, died on July 12, 1948. He had worked harmoniously with the directors and had led his institution safely and conservatively through a period of slow but steady growth. The directors noted his service in the following resolution: "We, who knew Dick Barton as a friend, as a business associate and a constant companion are profoundly grieved by his passing. His works, his ideals, and his genial spirit are still with us, and will remain as a beacon to help guide us on our course, though the captain's hand has been taken from the wheel."

It seems that this loss was anticipated by the

Board of Directors, for one month before Barton's death they had employed a new executive vice president who was promptly elevated to fill the vacant position of president.

The eighth president of the bank was William B. Pollard. Like all previous presidents, he was not educated in banking; but unlike all of them, he had accumulated a varied record of practical banking experience by the time of his appointment at the age of 52. Born at Chester, Mississippi, in 1896, he graduated from high school and attended Mississippi State College at Starkville for a time before beginning his business career. He served as a clerk at banks in Hattiesburg and Jackson until he became a soldier during World War I. Returning to his native state after the war, he took a position as officer for a lumber manufacturing company, but left this employment to own and operate his own store in Ackerman.

Beginning in 1927, he resumed his banking career as a bank examiner for the Mississippi State Banking Department. During the next six years, he made many friends among bankers in the northern area of his state, the part nearest to the business influence of Memphis. In 1933, he became an assistant examiner for the Board of Governors of the Federal Reserve System in Washington. After advancing steadily through a series of positions, he was elected in 1946 as a vice president of the Federal Reserve Bank of St. Louis. This was the headquarters of the Eighth Federal Reserve District,

William B. Pollard

including all or part of seven states. He was assigned as manager of the Memphis branch of the Federal Reserve Bank. In this position, he developed a working acquaintance with hundreds of bankers across the Mid-South area. It was this record of experience that led the directors of National Bank of Commerce to employ him as a successor to Richard Barton.

As president of the bank, William B. Pollard was to manage the institution through the remainder of the Forties and through most of the new decade of the Fifties. He obviously possessed valuable experience and skill in supervising the internal affairs of the business. Personable and well liked by the bank employees, he also brought with him the friendship of many other bankers throughout the area served by his bank. Since his background was in an essentially rural region and the Eighth Federal Reserve District had emphasized service to agriculture, he worked effectively in strengthening the customary position of National Bank of Commerce as the major financial supporter of Mid-South agriculture. Aware of the danger of too much reliance on the production of a single crop, and apparently able to foresee some of the impending problems of the cotton industry, he became a strong advocate of diversified farming, livestock raising, and soil conservation. Active in the affairs of his city, he assumed executive positions in the Chamber of Commerce, the Shelby County Community Chest, the board of trustees of John Gaston Hospital, the Memphis Amateur Athletic

Union, the local chapter of the American Red Cross, and the Memphis Council of the Navy League.

It seems clear, however, that the influence of President William Pollard on the policies of the bank, like that of his predecessor and his successor, was overshadowed by the strong personality of the chairman of the Board of Directors, William R. King. In fact, it appears that King wielded a dominant influence over the course followed by the bank during the third of a century prior to his death in 1965. He maintained his interest in the bank as long as he lived. Unlike many officers, who preferred to work in private offices, he kept his desk behind one of the columns in the main lobby where he could greet his many friends who entered and keep a watchful eye on all the activities of the institution.

This powerful control William King exercised was invaluable during the first years of recovery from the panic and the run on the bank, but later it was apparently detrimental to the growth and progress needed during a highly competitive era. Described by an officer who knew him affectionately and well as "the tightest man I ever knew," King was a prudent and cautious banker. Customers could rest assured that he would take no risks with their funds. And there is no question that he loved his city, his bank, and the traditions of both. Basically, the problem was that the nation, the economy, and the city changed around him, but he did not want the bank to change.

The years following World War II were characterized by sustained economic expansion, increasing population, a rising level of affluence, and a proliferation of automobile ownership. These factors produced a great migration out of Memphis to the suburbs. Retail businesses followed the movement, and the construction of new suburban shopping centers began. As the downtown area began to decline as a business center, First National Bank and Union Planters National Bank began the building of branch banks.

But National Bank of Commerce remained resistant to change. It had opened a drive-in teller's window

at the main office earlier in the 1940s, and on September 15, 1948, it made a tentative single entry into branch banking by opening the Gilmore branch at Madison Avenue and McLean Street. The sturdy Gilmore Building was a tower similar to downtown structures. The branch was on the ground floor of this building, but a worse site could hardly have been found. Located too near the downtown area to be of much convenience to suburban residents, it had a limited number of parking spaces. It was later moved to another location.

The change to branch banking came only after much delay and considerable urging by a new director, a young World War II veteran, Robert G. Snowden. He later recounted one of his conversations with King, who said, "Young man, I don't know whether we are going to have any branch banks. We like to have people come down here. We have the best banking quarters in Memphis and we want them to come down here. We have fine offices and we could really take care of them. I don't like this branch banking." The matter was resolved later after Snowden submitted his resignation from the Board of Directors. King refused to accept the resignation and tore up the letter Snowden gave him, but during the Fifties he did allow a limited beginning of branch banking.

It should be understood that this resistance to change was the prevailing policy of National Bank of Commerce, which had an unusually long continuity of leadership. Many of the directors, officers, and stockholders had memories of the near loss of their institution and were equally committed to a cautious and tried policy of operation. The bank was sound. It had survived and it had operated at a profit. In Snowden's words about William King, "He had built a good mousetrap and it was working." The problem was that by this time others had built better mousetraps, and they were working more effectively. The net result was that the bank was steadily losing ground in its competition for the financial business of Memphis and the Mid-South.

September 15, 1948, National Bank of Commerce made a tentative single entry into branch banking by opening the Gilmore branch at Madison Avenue and McLean Street.

The trends of the late Forties continued into the decade of the Fifties. Memphians of this decade lived in a fortunate time and place. Farming had become more diversified so that the region was less dependent on cotton. By this time the Bluff City participated more fully in the national economy, which had become quite favorable. At the beginning of this decade, the United States had entered a postwar period of continued expansion that lasted without interruption for a generation. In Memphis jobs were more numerous than at any other time except during World War II, and wages climbed steadily. The rate of inflation remained low so that the standard of living rose throughout this era. Both large and small businesses prospered as a result of this affluence.

Housing opportunities improved for most city residents. Slum clearance and the building of housing developments with federal funds reduced the large

number of substandard units that had been widespread in Memphis. For those with money, large numbers of subdivisions were being developed with prices that met the budgets of most workers. City maps for the decade show a regular move eastward of residential areas.

The influence of land developers over the political leaders in Memphis was strong. Almost all requests for subdivision were approved without question. Large areas of new homes were filled in east of Highland and north of Poplar. What was then the southeast corner of the city began to be settled east of Getwell and south of Park Avenue.

Memphis had grown to 396,000 people by 1950, an increase of more than 100,000 in a decade. Most of this growth actually took place beyond the city limits; the city annexed 65 square miles in the late 1940s, taking in about 75,000 people. The automobile made this suburban growth possible. Registrations of vehicles increased through the decade. Advertisements in the newspapers show a strong market for both new and used cars. The general prosperity made it possible for the first time for even young people to drive their own cars. In fact, an entire culture built around the automobile appeared. Many current citizens of the city remember the large number of drive-in movies and restaurants of the decade.

By the Fifties, the city was frequently winning awards that reflected an improved appearance as well as the growing economy. In 1950 and in 1951 it won the award as the "Nation's Cleanest City." In 1957, Memphis received the award for "Nation's Quietest City" for the 17th time. By the close of the decade it had received the *Look* magazine award for urban renewal and was rated second in the national Inter-Chamber Fire Safety Contest.

Fire insurance rates were low in the city and police protection was effective. Organized prostitution and gambling had finally been driven out before the beginning of World War II. The crime rate was low and the tradition of the rough river town that had been the murder capital of the nation was being forgotten. The use of narcotics apparently was lower than it had been or was to be subsequently during the century, and most citizens did not consider crime to be a major problem. Many of the efforts of the police were directed toward the increasing traffic problem.

A public works project of great economic importance developed during this decade. Presidents Island, an area of about 1,000 acres, had always been connected with the history of Memphis, but was accessible only by boat. Federal funds were secured from Congress to build a dam and a causeway to connect the upper end of it with the eastern bank of the river. On October 9, 1950, the dam was completed. The large island thus became available as an area for industrial expansion. The closure of the channel also provided a harbor of calm water for barge traffic serving firms that took advantage of the new location.

The sustained diversification of the economy dur-

ing this era included the development of Memphis as a wholesale center serving an extensive area of the Mid-South. Wholesale operations out of the city had been a business activity from the early years, but they had been tied mainly to the cotton trade. The sources of the cotton that flowed into the Bluff City had received their supplies in a return exchange. By the Fifties, wholesale suppliers of almost all products retailed in the towns of the Mid-South operated from the city. According to *Sales Management Magazine*, Memphis had a total of wholesale sales amounting to $1,335,243,000 annually. It was the largest wholesale city in the South and occupied 10th place in the nation.

Suburban expansion brought opportunities for business growth outside the traditional downtown area. The pioneer in this movement was Lowenstein's Department Store with the development of Poplar Plaza Shopping Center in 1949. This location at Poplar and Highland had previously been farmland. The Lowenstein family had long been associated with and done their banking at National Bank of Commerce. Whitehaven Plaza was started soon afterward, and many other new shopping centers soon began to be constructed.

In 1952, businessman Kemmons Wilson, who saw the trend away from the center of cities, built a motel, named Holiday Inn, on Summer Avenue. He was joined the following year by builder Wallace Johnson. This Memphis enterprise assessed the changes of the decade correctly, and within a generation, Holiday Inns became a symbol for travelers and an international business empire. Wallace Johnson was a customer of National Bank of Commerce.

An interesting feature of the Fifties was that the two most widely known persons who ever lived in Memphis both received conspicuous recognition during the decade. The first of these was Edward H. Crump, whose unique era came to an end at this time. By the date of his death in 1954, he had built the most powerful political machine that ever existed in Tennessee and had become one of the most noted political bosses in the history of the nation.

Crump had become the unquestioned ruler of politics in Memphis and Shelby County. From the latter part of the Thirties his organization also dominated state politics. The official capital of Tennessee remained in Nashville, but the real center of political power in the state was at Main and Adams in Memphis. From his office there, Crump — "The Man on the Corner," as the newspapers and members of his organization called him — directed the course of Tennessee. During the time of his greatest influence, his choice alone determined who would be governor of the state, and his political organization dominated all branches of its government.

This power gave Memphis influence in Washington during the last decades of his life. Crump lost no opportunity to bring state and federal funds to his city.

Although Elvis Presley received special attention as a customer of National Bank of Commerce, it was consistent with the bank's long-standing tradition of attempting to provide personalized service to all its customers.

One Nashville political observer noted that during the Crump era, "Memphis alleys were better than Nashville streets." Although the Bluff City received many financial and material benefits from this political machine, it did not survive Crump's death. There was no other person who could fill his role, and the organization was left without leadership. The center of political power in Tennessee shifted back to Nashville, where it has remained since.

During the afternoon of October 16, 1954, as

Crump, at the age of 80, lay dying in his home at 1962 Peabody Avenue, another Memphis resident, 19 years of age, was in Shreveport, Louisiana, preparing to appear that evening on the program "Louisiana Hayride." His name was Elvis Presley. One career was ending and another beginning. In 1954, every person in Memphis knew Edward Crump's name. Far fewer knew the name of Elvis Presley.

Different though they might have seemed, the two men had much in common. Both had limited formal education and had migrated to Memphis from Mississippi while still in their teens. Both became millionaires, and both achieved such fame and success that they would be commemorated with statues in their city. Yet by the time of Elvis Presley's death in 1977, the fame he had won surpassed that of any other person who ever lived in Memphis. Indeed, his name was probably known to more people throughout the world than any person who ever lived in the state of Tennessee — including the three of its citizens who became president of the United States. According to the obituary in *Variety* magazine, Presley's lifetime earnings totaled approximately $4.3 billion, including income from music, records, publishing commissions, movies, concerts, and the sale of souvenirs and memorabilia.

Elvis Presley's personal banking in Memphis was done at National Bank of Commerce. One of the bank's

The grand lobby of the main office of National Bank of Commerce was converted into an elegant dining hall for the employees' annual Christmas party, December 17, 1955.

officers, Clarence H. Carter, was a friend of Elvis and his father, Vernon. Gus B. Denton, now executive vice president at the bank, remembers that Carter was transferred to the Whitehaven branch where he could assist Elvis and his family with their banking. Although Elvis Presley received special attention, it was consistent with the bank's long-standing tradition of attempting to provide personalized service to all its customers.

In the history of National Bank of Commerce, the decade of the Fifties and the first half of the Sixties was a tranquil and pleasant time for those who worked for the institution. During this halcyon era, the employees shared many characteristics of a large and supportive family. Every July an annual employees picnic was given, usually at Rainbow Lake, and in December tables were decorated in the lobby for a gala Christmas

dinner and party. Every working day, free meals, prepared by skilled and experienced cooks, were served at noon to all employees. By 1954, 260 employees of the bank were being served in this cafeteria. The newest teller or stenographer was often able to have lunch with the president or other senior officers of the bank. There was familiarity and much genuine friendship among those who served the bank.

During this stable and peaceful era, it was almost as if the venerable institution existed in a time warp from a past age. In fact, many employees had spent a lifetime in the service of their bank. On June 2, 1951, Leslie A. Thornton, a vice president, was honored for having given 50 years of service — having begun his career with the start of the century. James L. Ross, who became president during the decade, had served under four of the eight presidents of the bank from the time he first began his employment as a young file clerk. He arrived for work early every day and seldom left the building during working hours, habits that were probably observed by many other bank officers.

The pace of activity was leisurely and the bank did not pursue an aggressive policy of competition with the other financial institutions of the city. But it was sound and profitable. It maintained its position as the world's largest cotton bank and relied heavily on its commercial lending division for profitability. It did not compete actively for the retail side of banking in the city. Directors John D. Canale, Jr. and Robert G. Snowden, who were involved with the bank during this era, remember a strong emphasis on service to long-standing accounts in real estate, cotton, groceries, and lumbering. These major businesses provided much of the success of the commercial lending division.

Although National Bank of Commerce operated conservatively and profitably from its headquarters in the finest business building in the city, there was nothing modern about it. Wayne W. Pyeatt, who arrived as executive vice president at the end of this era, has the following recollection: "I was absolutely shocked that the bank could have existed as long as it had...let's say from 1940 to 1965...with as little knowledge as was involved. There was nothing up-to-date about it. The people were paid zero. People did things the way they had always done...It was run by people who had been there a long time and were elderly at that time and they really knew nothing about it. The files were not complete. I found after I had been there the first year, I guess, the lending officers were getting rather substantial gifts at Christmas time, like four or five suits of clothes, a case of whiskey. I could not believe this kind of thing occurred. We stopped it and one of the officers, when I inquired about it, said Mr. Ross had felt that he would pay them a very small amount and whatever they made outside the bank was their affair."

Wayne Pyeatt was the first person ever to serve as president of the institution who had received an educa-

tion in banking. The shock that an educated, young bank officer in the 1960s would experience on arriving at this backward institution that was almost a relic from the past is understandable, but the bank did have some strengths in its tradition-encrusted structure. The fact that most of the loans were large ones to businesses well known to the bank officers and directors assured that very few bad loans were ever made, even without modern credit record keeping. And the strong loyalty of most officers, despite their low salaries, apparently kept them honest. Only one case of minor embezzlement by a teller, in September 1959, was reported during the era. It may well be that the custom of keeping financial activity reduced in scope also limited the possibility of making mistakes in lending and investments. Director W. Neely Mallory, Jr., who knew these bankers who had survived the Depression, observed that, "Their mind-set was preservation of capital. That is how they operated." While this era was not a time of growth for the bank, it was one in which few errors were made and no significant losses took place.

During this quiet era between two turbulent times in the bank's history, much of its true character can be observed. Director Emeritus Lucius E. Burch, Jr. who was present during these years, described it: "Banks do have characters of their own and NBC has one and it is of long-standing. NBC was always a bank that a very large part of its business was with the established companies and families of this area...There was an intimacy. A large part of the credit was extended on personal knowledge, believing that somebody would do the best they could, that when you got a warehouse receipt there would be a bale of cotton behind it. The bank has always been a highly personalized, conservative, no get-rich-quick schemes, no business of going out and buying up iffy mortgages and bundling them up and selling them. It is remarkably clean about that. The people that have been on the board of the bank, pretty generally, have been people that have known their families and have known each other for years and years and years — people like Elias Goldsmith and

The Hollywood branch of National Bank of Commerce, 2477 Chelsea Avenue, 1958.

people like that. It is a bank that has personality."

The volume of the bank's business increased gradually during this era, and some changes requiring capital expenditure and new personnel took place. In 1955, a renovation of the main building was completed. Costing $50,000, these improvements opened space on the third floor for the installment loan department and the bank cafeteria, which had previously been located in the basement level. The new cafeteria included a private dining room, lined with walnut paneling, for the entertainment of guests of the bank. The space then available in the basement was opened for storage and the use of other departments needing additional room.

Although the institution was late in beginning branch banking, it expanded gradually but steadily during these years. In 1952, the Chelsea branch, later called the Hollywood branch, was opened at Chelsea and Bryan, and the Lamar-Bellevue branch was opened at 1192 Lamar Avenue. Two years later, the pioneer Gilmore branch was moved to its own building at Madison and Barksdale, and this opening was followed within a year by the Mallory Heights branch at

East Mallory and Third. The Poplar-Perkins branch was opened in 1958, and the next year the Oakville branch was completed at 3856 Lamar. In 1961, the Whitehaven branch opened for business at 3338 Highway 51 South, and a new "Motor Bank" was added at 55 South Second Street for the use of downtown customers who wished to transact business from their automobiles. The following year, the Summer Avenue branch, at 5121 Summer, opened; and during the next three years, two new branches were completed, the Frayser branch at 3686 North Watkins Street, and the Jackson Avenue branch at 3232 Jackson. By 1965, the Poplar-Perkins branch was called the Laurelwood branch, and the original Gilmore branch had been moved to 1895 Union Avenue where it was called the Union Avenue-Gilmore branch.

The development of the bank during this period of the Fifties and early Sixties is revealed by information from the annual reports. In the 1955 report, it listed total resources and liabilities of $118,065,780.81, and deposits of $110,121,447.23. Five years later, the 1960 annual report gave resources and liabilities of

$131,383,741.22, and deposits of $117,382,611.60. The 1965 annual report listed total assets and liabilities of $178,157,601.91, and deposits of $155,793,113.97.

Another change in the formal leadership of National Bank of Commerce took place during the latter part of the Fifties. On July 11, 1957, President William B. Pollard died at the age of 61 as the result of a heart attack. His successor was James L. Ross who at the time was serving as an executive vice president of the institution. Having started work as a file clerk at the age of 18, Ross had spent a lifetime in the service of the bank. With the approval of his employers, he had taken leave to complete his education in order to further his career. He attended the University of Mississippi, graduated from the University of Tennessee in 1923, and later graduated from the University of Memphis Law School and was admitted to the bar. However, he returned to the bank and served in the trust department and the bond department. Promoted through a succession of positions, he had served as executive vice president since 1949. It was his responsibility after 1957 to provide formal leadership for the institution, but his presidency brought no substantive changes from those of Richard Barton and William Pollard. In fact, it did not particularly matter which person served as president during this era, for the bank was dominated by William King from his position on the Board of Directors. John D.

In keeping with America's love affair with the automobile in the 1950-60s, National Bank of Commerce's "Motor Bank" opened at 55 South Second Street in June 1961. Drive-in service allowed customers to transact business from their cars.

Canale, Jr., who remembers the bank from this era, described the relationship as follows: "Mr. King called the shots. No question about it."

For the city of Memphis, the decade of the Sixties brought a time of dynamic growth and change. The population increased from 497,524 in 1960 to 623,530 in 1970, and its nature became more cosmopolitan as an increasing number of people moved into the city from other parts of the country. Also, events related to the civil rights movement strongly affected Memphis during the Sixties as desegregation came to the public schools under the supervision of the federal courts. Virtually all aspects of business and public life became integrated by the time the decade was over. Not all the changes came peacefully. The assassination of Dr. Martin Luther King at the Lorraine Motel on April 4, 1968, brought widespread violence but also initiated the process of bringing many white and black leaders together to address the racial problems that had traditionally characterized Memphis.

The downtown business district, the historic heart of the city, was strongly affected by two contradictory developments in this era. One was a renaissance of urban construction in the area; the other was an increasing movement of people away from this center of the city.

This decade changed the skyline of Memphis. The highest building in the city was completed in 1966, the

38-story 100 North Main Building. It rose 450 feet above ground level. The First Tennessee Bank Building at Madison and Third also provided new office space. The Shelby County Administration Building was constructed in 1960, and was soon followed by the Federal Building, a new Memphis City Hall, and the Tennessee State Office Building. These structures, together with Ellis Auditorium — soon to become Cook Convention Center — served as an anchor to the downtown through the next two decades. Their example was needed, for private businesses and residential housing continued to decline.

The people continued to move toward the ever-expanding suburbs, and the reigning department stores and specialty shops downtown, as well as the restaurants that had served their customers, all experienced hard times. Goldsmith's, Oak Hall, Gerber's, Julius Lewis, York Arms, and others that had kept their clientele for a generation followed the example of Lowenstein's and began to move operations toward the outskirts of the city. Financial institutions also found it necessary to transfer their operations to where the people were. By 1960, National Bank of Commerce had six branches, but Union

James L. Ross

Planters National Bank had 20, while First National Bank had started an aggressive branch expansion that would make it the largest bank in the city by the close of the decade.

The focus of National Bank of Commerce during the first half of the Sixties was still on the downtown area, which was becoming increasingly empty. The heart of Memphis had not been so abandoned since the yellow fever epidemic of the 1870s. Director Emeritus Walter P. Armstrong, Jr., whose law firm worked on the development of Southland Mall, observed that this mall and other new suburban shopping centers "withdrew the center of activity from downtown and dispersed it to a number of outlying areas with the result of a certain amount of deterioration in the downtown area." Director Emeritus Robert G. Snowden, who was involved in real estate at the time, commented, "You could shoot down the street in the Sixties and not hit anybody." Despite the great changes that were taking place in the city, the bank passed through the first half of the decade with little alteration of its traditional customs.

Under the new presidency of Lewis K. McKee, National Bank of Commerce began preparation for Commerce Square, a 32-story financial and business complex connected to the west side of the bank's headquarters building. Pictured here is an architectural rendering by Roy P. Harrover and Associates.

CHAPTER SEVEN

INTO THE BOLD YEARS: BANKING IN A DYNAMIC AND TROUBLED DECADE

In some respects, the year 1965 was as crucial in the history of National Bank of Commerce as the year 1933 had been. In 1965, the bank experienced a near revolutionary change of leadership. When the year began, President James L. Ross was dying after a lingering illness, and William R. King, whose powerful influence had dominated the institution for over three decades, was in declining health at the age of 87. At this time he was in the final 100 days of his life. The executive vice president, L. E. Wittenberg, who, according to Director Rudi Scheidt, had actually been running the bank, had retired two months previously after 38 years of service.

Understanding the necessity for new leadership, the Board of Directors had made plans for succession. James L. Ross died on January 18, 1965, and was replaced three days later by Lewis Kavanaugh McKee who had been brought to the bank as a vice president in 1963 and promoted to executive vice president in November 1964. It was certainly time for new leadership and a change of direction for the institution. From its modest beginning, the bank had become the largest and most successful financial firm in Memphis. Then, following the near loss in 1933, it had survived, and had indeed maintained profitability, but it had become locked into policies of rigidity and caution. It had been surpassed by far by its competitors. If a change of course could not be made, it might continue to survive as a sound, small bank, but it would fall even further behind the major banks of the city. The policies it had followed were insufficient for the times. Their effect, as described by Robert G. Snowden, were: "We were going to be cut out completely. We would have been just a little country bank in the heart of downtown Memphis."

Lewis McKee, who served as president from 1965 until 1969, and remained as chairman of the Board of Directors until 1974, was one of the strongest, and also one of the most controversial, leaders National Bank of Commerce ever had. Some of the new activities he initiated were successful, some are still debatable, and others may have been mistakes — but he did make changes — and under his administration the bank finally entered the modern age. Despite the turmoil that ensued as a result of some of his decisions, the net effect for the bank was probably positive, for after the tumult subsided and stability was once again achieved, the bank entered its greatest era of expansion and profitability.

Lewis McKee became president at a time the employees recognized a need for new leadership. According to Wayne Pyeatt, who worked with McKee, "They were very good people. They just lacked leadership. They were anxious to be led. When Lewis came in, they thought everything was going to be wonderful because here was this new man who all of them knew by reputation...and he is going to lead us and he did, and they loved him."

Personable, educated, handsome, and persuasive, McKee was a natural leader of others. If there is such a quality as luck, he had it, although it is possible that sometimes the force of a personality produces its own fortune. Robert G. Snowden described it thus: "It is often said about Lewis, you could throw him off the top of the Falls Building and he would light in a bucket of water and not even get wet." John D. Canale, Jr.'s description was, "Man, you fall in the gutter and come up with a fish in your pocket." There seems to have been no question of the new president's ability and charisma, even by those who came into bitter conflict with him.

A successful partner in the Lytle McKee Cotton Company, he had no experience in banking except as a member of the Board of Directors of Union Planters National Bank, with which his family had long been associated. He gave up that position when he was persuaded to come to National Bank of Commerce. Active in the social and civic life of Memphis, he was personally acquainted with many of the most successful business owners of the city. He served as president of the Memphis Cotton Exchange, the Memphis County Club, as treasurer of the Shelby United Neighbors, and as an officer or active member of many other community organizations. These activities had given him such newspaper attention that he was one of the best known citizens of the city.

Changes in the bank began to be made immediately. His wide acquaintance with members of the business community enabled him to acquire a substantial number of commercial accounts, and he also started a new program of expansion of facilities that soon added five new branches to serve residents of the suburban areas. In 1966, National Bank of Commerce expanded by acquiring a smaller financial institution, State Savings

Lewis Kavanaugh McKee

Bank. During the same year, he introduced the first bank credit card, the Charge-All, which was converted two years later to an interbank card, the MasterCharge. Despite some initial doubts about the security of this new credit, it was soon announced in an annual report that the credit card operation had become "one of our most profitable services."

Innovations were adopted at a rapid pace. An investment division was formed in 1966, and during the following year National Bank of Commerce became the first in the city to have commercial accounts and correspondent banks on a data processing system. A transition of the bank's entire record keeping to computers was completed soon afterward. In 1966, an employee profit sharing plan was inaugurated, and in 1967 the bank became the first in Memphis to offer daily interest on savings accounts. The bank led the local financial community in increasing the interest rate on savings to 4 percent. During this era, a business development section and a marketing department were added. By 1969, the total number of branches opened had been increased to 18.

The two most conspicuous, and most controversial, innovations made by Lewis McKee as president were the construction of a new downtown skyscraper and the participation in a bank holding company. The new building, of course, was the indication of the institution's new status most visible to the public. Union Planters National Bank and First National Bank (later changed to First

Celebrating ground-breaking ceremonies in 1968 for the new Commerce Square complex were (from left) Wayne W. Pyeatt, Wayne Trumpf, Henry Loeb, and Lewis K. McKee.

Tennessee Bank) had tall new buildings that dominated the downtown skyline with their signs publicly displayed. Believing that National Bank of Commerce should also be represented by a similar tower, he began preparation for Commerce Square, a 32-story financial and business complex connected to the west side of the bank's headquarters building.

Designed by the noted architectural firm of Roy P. Harrover and Associates, it was modern in its structure and probably the most aesthetically impressive skyscraper in Memphis. Abe Plough, a millionaire investor and associate of the bank, worked through a dummy corporation to acquire the land needed for the building, and the bank demolished an inadequate parking garage it had previously built in order to secure space for the larger one

necessary for the new complex. Construction started in 1968, the bank moved into its space on the second, fourth, fifth, sixth, and seventh floors at the end of 1972, and the remainder of the building was opened for tenants the following year.

Problems, both in construction and finance, were experienced during the completion of this project. A very deep excavation was necessary, an underground spring was discovered underneath the site, and expensive shoring work was necessary to prevent damage to adjacent building walls.

Financial problems were even more troublesome, and the tower ultimately cost the bank considerably more than expected. The original estimate was that the cost of the building would be approximately $14 million,

An aerial view of Commerce Square tower and garage, under construction, shows their proximity to the existing National Bank of Commerce headquarters building.

of which the bank would be responsible for 25 percent. Initially, the plan was that Plough, Inc. would share the use of the building with the bank; but during the development of the project, Plough decided instead to construct its own building on Jackson Avenue. Northwestern Mutual Company and Wallace Johnson were also to share in the cost of the new tower. But Johnson, a commercial borrower of the bank, experienced major business reverses which caused the bank to have to exchange the debt for his equity in the tower. Due to these subsequent problems, the bank's initial planned investment of $3.5 million ultimately totaled $10 million in capital committed to the new building.

The wisdom of the decision to construct the new tower is debatable. From a purely financial perspective, it may well have been a mistake. The building did tie up a large amount of capital that could have otherwise been used much more profitably, and the new space needed for banking operations could have been acquired elsewhere at considerably less expense. Walter P. Armstrong, Jr.'s observation is, "It became somewhat of a white elephant on the hands of the bank, I think, and there was a very definite move to withdraw the bank's ownership in the tower."

There were other considerations, however, in addition to the financial ones. W. Neely Mallory's view is, "I would say the construction of the tower was a statement that, if nothing else, we were no longer going to be a sleepy bank in Memphis, but we were going to try to be a growing, important financial institution here."

The analysis of Bruce E. Campbell, Jr., then executive vice president of the bank is that: "It gave us a landmark. I think it was the tail end of an era when banks built huge facilities, signature buildings. A lot of building went on after that, but I am thinking about people who basically should have known better. Banking does not need to be in such quarters. It is a low margin business, and in this day and time should be done in low margin quarters."

The decision to involve National Bank of Commerce in a bank holding company was made by Lewis McKee, but the organization he decided to join had been previously formed by an East Tennessee banker, William B. Greene. In the late 1960s, the formation of bank holding companies under the federal Bank Holding Company Act of 1956 had become increasingly popular primarily as a method to avoid state statutes restricting intrastate branching.

The bank holding company that William Greene formed was the Tennessee Financial Corporation, organized on February 18, 1966. Later that year it acquired substantially all of the stock of the First Peoples Bank at Johnson City, and in April 1967 the stock in Carter County Bank at Elizabethton, Tennessee.

Wayne W. Pyeatt's recollection of Lewis McKee's discovery of William Greene's holding company is as follows: "It just fascinated Lewis. They were from far East Tennessee — Elizabethton and Johnson City. Lewis went to see him. The guy was very personable. Lewis is person-

The bank moved into its new space in Commerce Square at the end of 1972, and the remainder of the building was opened for tenants the following year.

able and they hit it off like nobody's business. So the first thing you know, we joined hands...Lewis, and I mean just Lewis on this hand, and the people who were involved in these other banks joined together almost as a friendship, a social thing. 'Wouldn't it be great if we all got together and we will have this big bank?'"

In retrospect, it is possible to say that the decision to bring National Bank of Commerce into the holding company was, as Bruce E. Campbell, Jr., analyzes it, done without sufficient deliberation: "The way it evolved was too casual to be a good business proposition for the long term. It seemed like a way to increase the size, but little forethought had been given to the implications of company board control and opportunities, through consolidation, to make more money."

But Lewis McKee was persuasive, and there were some advantages that were obvious to the directors. It did give the bank a new opportunity to expand its operations. W. Neely Mallory's recollection is: "I would say philosophically I was very much in favor of it because growing the size of NBC within the Memphis business community, this trade area, was certainly not an easy task. First Tennessee and UP were very strong, so any market share we gained was a bloody fight. It seemed to me that branching out into other areas gave the stockholders of the bank a chance to grow the size of the bank through some acquisitions. And, I guess, in theory there are savings that should have inured to the operating side of the bank as a result of that."

A majority of the directors were convinced and the decision was made. In June 1970, Tennessee Financial Corporation changed its name to United Tennessee Bancshares Corporation. In May 1971, the shareholders of National Bank of Commerce, Memphis, exchanged substantially all of their outstanding shares for stock in United Tennessee Bancshares Corporation, and National Bank of Commerce became the third bank under the holding company umbrella. Walter P. Armstrong described the change: "I remember at the time the holding company was formed, that it was necessary for the holding company to own a controlling share of National Bank of Commerce stock. This was relatively simple because fortunately a large amount of the NBC stock was owned by people who lived in Shelby County and a lot of it by people on the Board of Directors. Of course, being in favor of this, they willingly turned over their shares."

Thus National Bank of Commerce began a new phase of its history as part of the UTBC bank holding company. These three banks were joined by Nashville City Bank and Trust Company in December 1971 and First Trust and Savings Bank at Paris, Tennessee, in October 1972. The five banks that comprised United Tennessee Bancshares Corporation extended geographically from extreme upper East Tennessee through Middle Tennessee and ultimately to the most southwestern corner of the state. Unfortunately, the disparities in geography brought with it disparities in representation on United Tennessee Bancshares Corporation's board of directors and, more importantly, what eventually proved to be irreconcilable differences in management philosophies and objectives. For the next five years, the five banks attempted to work under this holding company structure, but UTBC board meetings became increasingly fractious. National Bank of Commerce, Memphis, and its directors on the UTBC holding company board found the philosophical gulf separating them from their affiliates ever widening.

The trouble that led to conflict between Memphis directors and a faction of other members of the UTBC holding company board was not caused by any mismanagement or financial losses on the part of National Bank of Commerce. Events in Nashville initiated the difficulty. Nashville City Bank and Trust Company suffered a loss of about $4 million of its capital as a result of activities in which it had become involved. This loss not only left the Nashville bank unable to contribute dividend payments to the stockholders of United Tennessee Bancshares Corporation, but made it necessary for UTBC to secure a large loan in order to rescue its unprofitable member institution. The disparity between the profitable Memphis institution and the troubled Nashville bank emphasized and increased the differences of interest among members of the holding company board.

In February 1974, a group of Jackson, Mississippi, investors led by Leland Speed, claiming to represent 15 percent of the stock of National Bank of Commerce exchanged for UTBC stock, requested representation on the UTBC board. Subsequently, in April of that year, J. Will Young, a Jackson, Mississippi, attorney, was elected to the board to represent their interests. The UTBC board of directors then consisted of Lewis McKee, chairman, and fellow Memphians John D. Canale, Jr. and Wayne Pyeatt; Nashvillians Calvin Houghland and Jack Massey; East Tennesseans Bill Greene and Oris Hyder; T. J. Weaver, Paris, and J. Will Young. A month later, in May 1974, Lewis McKee resigned as chairman of the board of directors but remained as a director. J. Will Young succeeded him as chairman. At a special meeting of the UTBC board in June, it accepted McKee's resignation as both a member of its board of directors and president of National Bank of Commerce.

The departure of Lewis McKee was a significant event in an increasingly trying struggle between the UTBC directors representing National Bank of Commerce, who sought to maintain control over their institution, and the coalition of East Tennessee, Nashville, and Mississippi directors who, having secured numerical control of the board of directors of the holding company, attempted to dominate the Memphis bank. The pressure brought to bear on all the Memphis directors who served both the UTBC holding company and the bank was intense. Wayne Pyeatt's recollection is that after an especially difficult ordeal, "Lewis left the next day. Just walked out. Lewis felt that he was just not going to put up with that kind of foolishness." Whatever the exact circumstances may have been, a turbulent era in the history of the bank came to an end.

Despite the problems with the holding company he had helped to create, and which, in the view of many associated with National Bank of Commerce, was to be the greatest danger it ever faced, Lewis McKee had accomplished much during his administration. He led the bank through a necessary break with its outdated customs and into a new era of innovation and growth. He also did much to help his city in the area of race relations. One of his bank officers provided the following recollection: "Martin Luther King was killed in 1968 which threw the bank into the middle of efforts to try to raise many millions of dollars which we helped do, and to try to bring the city forward. Lewis was primary in that effort." He is also given credit by a banker at a rival institution for being the first in Memphis to hire citizens of African-American descent for managerial positions in his bank.

Perhaps his greatest contribution was to the future leadership of the bank. He had the strength and self-confidence to bring in individuals of exceptional ability to serve with him. When he took over the management of the bank, it had never been led by men educated in banking. Lacking education and experience in banking himself, and seeing the need for these qualities, he brought in two professionally educated executives who themselves would later assume the leadership of the institution — Wayne W. Pyeatt and Bruce E. Campbell, Jr.

Many other young officers were recruited during the administration of Lewis McKee, and they also contributed their professionalism to the successful management of the various departments of the institution. McKee's influence thus continued constructively long after his service to the bank was completed.

The most obvious feature of National Bank of Commerce between 1965 and 1974 was change. It was a much different institution in 1974 from the one it had been nine years previously. There is no doubt that it had entered a period of rapid growth and had become a larger and more successful firm in spite of the controversy in which it was engaged. The expansion of suburban branch facilities to a total of 18 locations gave a visible presence of thriving business success throughout the metropolitan area, while the new downtown tower provided tangible proof that National Bank of Commerce had again become a major competitor for a share of the Memphis banking market. The adoption of the first bank credit card, the creation of the investment division, the payment of interest computed daily, the employee profit sharing plan, and the computerization of records had all attracted favorable notice. An even more important contribution than any of these innovations was the great public and professional respect Lewis McKee brought when he came to the bank. In the era immediately preceding his arrival, the bank staff had no officers who could meet on a peer level with the most prominent business leaders of the city. McKee's arrival had given the institution an executive with the ability to deal both on a social and a professional level with all of them.

With the departure of Lewis McKee in 1974, the formal leadership of the bank passed to Wayne W. Pyeatt, who actually had been managing most of the operations of the bank since his arrival as executive vice president in February 1966. Pyeatt also inherited the ongoing ordeal of the struggle between his bank and its holding company. The son of a banker, he grew up in Fayetteville, Arkansas. Following service in World War II, he graduated from the University of Arkansas and then joined his father who at the time owned the Searcy Bank in Searcy, Arkansas. Leaving work to attend the Stonier Graduate School of Banking at Rutgers University, he received his certificate in banking and returned to Searcy where he worked at the bank from 1948 until 1960. He then accepted a position as vice president of the First National Bank in Little Rock and was soon promoted to executive vice president, which position he held when Lewis McKee recruited him to come to Memphis to join National Bank of Commerce.

Since McKee was not a banker, and was mainly involved in activities outside of the bank, Pyeatt was placed in charge of virtually all banking operations except investments and the trust department. These responsibilities were handled so successfully that he was made president of the bank in 1969 when McKee moved up to become chairman of the Board of Directors. Pyeatt's professional training in banking was of great value to the institution during this era. He modernized banking operations by introducing the long overdue accrual accounting system, computerizing the records of the bank, increasing employees' salaries, improving the credit records, and introducing a system of providing professional training of bank officers through courses of the American Institute of Banking. In all of these improvements, he worked closely with Bruce E. Campbell, Jr., also a professionally educated banker, who joined the institution as a vice president in 1967, was named senior lending officer in 1968, and became executive vice president and a board member in 1971.

The value of Pyeatt's contributions to the bank was recognized by those who served with him. All uniformly praise his work in keeping the bank in operation and improving its efficiency during a difficult time. Robert G. Snowden described him as a professional who was "a

Wayne W. Pyeatt

very capable banker." W. Neely Mallory remembered that during his administration the institution became "a quieter bank, one that tended to stick to its knitting in the banking business, and maybe did not give as much effort to get in the paper perhaps or to show Memphis this is a new vibrant institution."

It was unfortunate that the administration of this capable and effective banker had to be conducted in an atmosphere of such turbulence and acrimony caused by the problem with the holding company. When McKee left in June 1974, he was replaced as UTBC director by Memphian W. Neely Mallory and Wayne Pyeatt was named chairman of National Bank of Commerce and vice chairman of UTBC. J. Will Young was elected president of UTBC. In November 1974, Pyeatt succeeded Young as president, and Young became chairman. The holding company began to unravel when William B. Greene re-acquired all of the stock of Carter County Bank and First Peoples Bank in October of that year for approximately $8.5 million in cash, yet remained a member of the UTBC board for another two years.

Thereafter, a bitter two-year struggle for control of UTBC and its three banks began in earnest. At the end of 1975, National Bank of Commerce with $446 million in assets was significantly larger and more profitable than its affiliates, the $99 million-asset Nashville City Bank and $24 million-asset First Trust and Savings Bank, Paris. Non-Memphians, led by Calvin Houghland, chairman, and fellow Nashvillians Jack C.

Massey, James A. Webb, Jr., and Thomas L. Cummings, along with East Tennessean William B. Greene, Jr., Paris representative Jack E. Veazey, Sr., Jackson, Mississippi, attorney J. Will Young, and Russell T. Cramer, a former Midwest thrift executive hired at the insistence of the Nashville contingent, continued to control the 15-member UTBC board. The remaining seven members of the board consisted of Memphians Wayne W. Pyeatt, W. Neely Mallory, Max B. Ostner, Sr., Donald Drinkard, James E. McGehee, Jr., John D. Canale, Jr. and Lucius E. Burch, Jr.

The difficulties between National Bank of Commerce and the UTBC holding company continued without apparent prospect of resolution, and on May 11, 1976, in a called meeting of the bank's Board of Directors, Wayne Pyeatt submitted his resignation. In a prepared statement, he said, "For some time I have not received the personal satisfaction from my work that I feel is necessary for me. Therefore, I have today resigned my position as chairman of the board and chief executive officer of National Bank of Commerce. I have also resigned as vice chairman and member of the board of directors of United Tennessee Bancshares Corporation."

The headline in *The Commercial Appeal* announced, "Dissatisfied Banker Quits NBC Top Job,"

The Board of Directors of National Bank of Commerce met and unanimously elected Bruce E. Campbell, Jr. as chairman of the board and chief executive officer in May 1976.

but Pyeatt had experienced no dissatisfaction with National Bank of Commerce. Two factors were involved. One was a recent family tragedy involving the loss of his daughter. The other was the unceasing struggle with the holding company which continued its effort to take control of the bank from its Memphis directors and officers. Pyeatt later reminisced, "It was a jaw to jaw fight and that was one of my problems. I did not see it ever ending. It was just going to go on and on and on, the constant bickering. I might, if I had not had that tragedy, have worked through it, but being completely frank about it all, I have been happier outside the business than I ever was in it."

But National Bank of Commerce, having survived for more than a century, was a continuing institution. Although the bank was involved in difficult problems, it was at the same time entering a time of great opportunity. New leadership was necessary, and it was quickly acquired. The Board of Directors met and unanimously elected Bruce E. Campbell, Jr. as chairman of the board and chief executive officer with the provision that he would also continue to serve as president. One era in the history of the bank was over and a new one, that would last until 1993, was beginning.

Bruce Emerson Campbell, Jr., 1993

CHAPTER EIGHT

THE BRUCE E. CAMPBELL, JR. YEARS:
THE COURSE UPWARD

Anew era in the life of National Bank of Commerce began on May 13, 1976, when Bruce E. Campbell, Jr. was elected as chairman of the board and chief executive officer of the institution. Having already served two years as the 12th president of the bank, he assumed the mantle of leadership at the age of 45 in a time of trouble, challenge, and great opportunity.

Born in Hattiesburg, Mississippi, he acquired his first banking experience by working as a runner for a local bank after school and on Saturdays. He came to Tennessee for his education at Vanderbilt University, from which he graduated with a B. A. degree in 1953. During this time, he spent a summer working at Marine Midland Bank in New York. Following graduation, he served four years as an officer in the United States Naval Reserve. Deciding to enter the profession of banking, he completed his studies, specializing in finance, at the Harvard University Graduate School of Business, and in 1959 the young M.B.A. graduate joined the Trust Company of Georgia in Atlanta. During his eight years there, he advanced from trainee to second vice president. Also, in 1966 he married Judith Fontaine of Jackson, Mississippi. The couple had two sons, Bruce E. Campbell, III and Carter F. Campbell.

His early success at the Trust Company of Georgia brought him to the attention of Lewis McKee, who, recognizing National Bank of Commerce's need for professionally educated banking executives with leadership ability, attempted to persuade him to come to Memphis. Successful in his position in Atlanta, Campbell declined McKee's offer in 1965. Two years later, the offer was repeated more persuasively and he and his wife, Judith, made the decision to move to

Memphis. Arriving in Memphis during the spring of 1967, he joined National Bank of Commerce as vice president of the lending division on April 10, 1967.

Campbell promptly and methodically analyzed the needs of the bank. Discovering a substantive need for improvements in the recruitment and training of personnel, he also found that the institution lacked a focused structure to credit and loan administration. Only sketchy financial information on borrowers had been assembled. Although the bank was strongly represented in the cotton business and several other commercial activities in the city, it lacked a representative cross section of Memphis businesses among its depositors. His conclusion was: "We had a lot of ground to cover: the staffing question, the training question, the focus question on what we were about and how to make good loans. Then we set about building a base of good, representative, Memphis commercial banking business."

His acute perception of the bank's needs and his vision of what the institution could become impressed Lewis McKee, Wayne Pyeatt, and the directors. His systematic and decisive action in changing the course of the bank in this new direction also gained their attention. In 1969, he was made first vice president of the lending division, and in the following year he became senior vice president and senior loan officer. In

1971, he was elected to membership on the National Bank of Commerce Board of Directors, and three years later he accepted complete responsibility for operations of the bank when he was elected president of the institution.

During these years, he assumed the various public duties customary for the leader of a major corporation. His professional standing was recognized by membership in Reserve City Bankers and on the board of the Tennessee Bankers Association. His community service included the board of trustees of Rhodes College, the board of trustees and executive committee of LeBonheur Children's Hospital, the board of Memphis Community Television Foundation, the Baptist Hospital advisory board, and the board of trustees of the William R. Moore School of Technology. Such professional and public service was expected of leaders of the bank, and he made valuable contributions in all these positions, but observers who knew him during these years agree that he was a banker's banker whose primary interest was always the progress of National Bank of Commerce.

When he first arrived at the bank, it had still not changed from its equipment and practices of the past. Many of the officers had been with the firm from an earlier era, and some of them still used snuff or chewing tobacco while working. His experience was, "Once you had a desk on the lending platform, you also were the proud possessor of a brass spittoon that was by every loan officer's desk. I thought this was a little curious, coming from Atlanta. I had trouble standing up and shaking hands with customers while trying to avoid my own spittoon." But changes from the ancient traditions were made, and under his direction the bank entered a new era of efficient operations, as modern as those of any other bank in the city.

Perhaps it is remarkable that any progress could be made at all, considering that National Bank of Commerce was still struggling for survival under a holding company board controlled by outsiders. This struggle, which had led to the termination of the services of his two predecessors, kept the future of the bank and all its employees in jeopardy for several years. It necessarily preoccupied the attention of the senior officers and directors. Understanding the absolute necessity of a display of confidence and courage by an effective leader, Campbell adopted the following policy: "We tried to shield the staff as much as possible from what was going on. It stopped with me. We would not let it show through in the terms of the day-to-day operation of the bank."

With an apparent confidence reminiscent of that of the Carthaginian general Hannibal when he viewed the Roman army before the Battle of Cannae, Campbell calmly directed the activities of his officers and employees. Inevitably, however, they became aware of the peril in which their institution had been placed. Wayne Pyeatt recalled, "When we had all the problems with the holding company, we could see they were worried. It was in the newspapers. They could see the rest of us were worried, and they were worried. It was a down time for everybody."

Nevertheless, the widely perceived danger brought everyone associated with the bank together in a unity that had not been seen since the great crisis of 1933, a time when the bank was almost lost 40 years previously. The resolution of the holding company problem was one of the great accomplishments of the Bruce Campbell administration, and it was one of the greatest victories in the history of National Bank of Commerce.

The problem was that National Bank of Commerce had surrendered its ownership to the holding company, United Tennessee Bancshares Corporation, which had become dominated by a majority of directors hostile to the independent control that the directors of the Memphis bank considered necessary to its continued survival. According to Director Lucius E. Burch, Jr., "They had the votes. The votes of the other banks could control what went on here." W. Neely Mallory, Jr. later explained the danger: "The concerns of the directors of NBC, I think, were that, one, they would all be fired, and that, two, in so doing the bank in Memphis could — destroyed is probably too strong a word — but would certainly have been damaged severely. A lot of the gilt-edged money that had been there for years and years would have been taken out."

If there is any error in Mallory's evaluation, it is probably on the side of modesty. Because of the unusually heavy commercial nature of the bank's accounts, most of its business was done with a relatively small number of large customers. The directors and those associated with them controlled a large enough percentage of the bank's business that its removal would either have destroyed the bank or reduced it to a hollow shell that would not have been profitable to the holding company.

Thus United Tennessee Bancshares Corporation had the power to crush the independence of National Bank of Commerce and impose outside management on the bank in any form it might wish — but it would have been a Pyrrhic victory, for the institution they would acquire would not be profitable. National Bank of Commerce was the holding company's only bank that produced substantial profits. As John D. Canale, later said, "They knew that NBC was the only bell cow they had. The other banks they had weren't doing worth a toot."

Hence the conflict was one which neither side could win, but neither side was willing to give up the struggle. In Lucius Burch's recollection, "The feeling between the Nashville bunch and the people here was intense." W. Neely Mallory remembers the impasse as, "...a stressful time...It was difficult to get out of it. We went through a period of time that wasn't much fun being on the board." Director Rudi Scheidt remembers accounts of all day meetings, all night meetings, and near fistfights that have left hard feelings for 20 years.

Despite several years of intense pressure, National Bank of Commerce, its directors, and its members on the board of the holding company refused to submit. As for the amount of authority they legally possessed,

Bruce Campbell remembered it as follows: "On paper, not that much. The stick of the control was clearly moved to the holding company where the bank did not have a majority vote. They had stacked the holding company board with non-Memphis folks. At one point, I think it was either seven or nine to four."

Nevertheless, the bank's directors fought to save the independence of their institution. They did have the handicap of doubts about the privacy or propriety of meeting in their own board room in their own bank to plan their strategy of defense. In W. Neely Mallory's recollection, "I don't know whether we thought the walls were bugged or not, but it just didn't seem like it was appropriate to use a holding company property to have a meeting that might be considered to be anti-holding company." Accordingly, they held meetings as needed away from the bank — at the Fischer Lime and Cement Company.

Facing the additional difficulty of being unable to use bank funds, which were also owned by the holding company, for their legal expenses, the Memphis directors contributed their own personal funds to retain the Atlanta law firm of King and Spalding. From this firm they secured the services of Bill Izlar, considered one of the area's most capable attorneys in dealing with similar corporate problems.

The struggle by National Bank of Commerce to retain its independence and deal with the takeover campaign consumed a great deal of time and effort. Accordingly, its Board of Directors appointed an ad hoc committee to coordinate its activities. Harry J. Phillips, Sr. was selected to be chairman and Michael McDonnell and W. Neely Mallory served as members. Phillips' recollection later was: "The board of directors of UTBC was being influenced by Nashville, East Tennessee, and Jackson, Mississippi, interests, so we decided to have an organized effort to secure controlling interest in our bank. We were selected by the National Bank of Commerce board to call the shots for the directors."

This committee took on the arduous but challenging and ultimately rewarding task of planning and directing the efforts to defend its bank. The responsibility required frequent and often lengthy meetings. The committee was indeed an ad hoc one, and certainly functioned without authority from the holding company, but its contributions were invaluable. The meetings were occasionally attended by the entire Board of Directors of the bank, and sometimes by whatever members were able to join them at the time.

An event that contributed to a settlement of the difficulty was the appointment of Memphis attorney Lucius E. Burch, Jr. to the board of directors of the holding company. Burch had been a long-time friend of Calvin Houghland, a leader of the Nashville group on the board of directors. The election of Burch to the board was at Houghland's request, but it was fortunate for all concerned, for he also had the respect and trust of the Memphis participants. W. Neely Mallory described his contribution: "Lucius did a wonderful job. I am not sure anybody else could have done it." Burch's own account of his efforts was more modest: "In the course of time, I was getting an easier case to plead with Calvin Houghland and the other banks. It was not hard really to convince them that they ought to be disillusioned with the marriage and the people here....We did break up the holding company, and I got credit for it to a degree quite disproportionate to what I deserved. The people in Memphis thought I had been the one that brought it about just because I was the one that brought the messages and did the talking in between, but it was the situation that everybody wanted."

It is always difficult to know what influences affect the action of others, but the decision by the non-Memphis members of the holding company's board was likely influenced by a secret initiative taken by John D. Canale, Jr. His account is as follows: "I hired a New York law firm to contact them and inform them that they had an anonymous investor (which was me) who wanted to buy out their blocks of stock. So I think that information prompted them to want to sell. They were afraid that somebody who might be very antago-

nistic to them was going to break up their playhouse...That made them even more nervous...They didn't know who in the heck it was. They knew somebody might come after them for a lot of things they had done that were bad — maybe an antagonistic other bank." Canale had previously received reports of dissention among the non-Memphis members of the board of the holding company, and it is possible that some members of the group involved in the takeover feared that others might dispose of their stock to the unidentified buyer who made the approach to them through the New York law firm.

Whatever the reasons for the decision to break up the holding company, there were many who had contributed their efforts to bring it about. Much of the credit for this victory was properly given to Bruce Campbell, for the agreement was reached within six months after his election to the UTBC holding company board. However, he gave credit to his NBC board: "The first thing we had was a wonderful board. We had a board that did not at that time own that much stock, but that stood awfully tall in terms of standing up for the bank and its people. I will never forget that. We have been blessed with a quality board all along, but they really shouldn't have had to be put through what our board was put through. They hung in there and in the end prevailed." W. Neely Mallory summarized it as, "a very trying time for the bank, and yet a time that brought together the officers and directors like one could hardly imagine. I think that is one of the strengths of the bank today."

Wayne Pyeatt attributed a substantial amount of the successful effort in defeating the takeover attempt to Bruce Campbell: "Bruce immediately moved. Within three months they unscrambled the egg. Everybody went his own way, took his stock back out of that situation...They were so tickled to see Lewis leave and then, two years later, they were so very pleased to see me leave, and when they went to see Bruce, he said, 'I am going to do exactly what the other two have been doing.' Finally they said, 'We give up.

How do we all get out of this thing?'...The bank board was 1,000 percent behind Lewis, behind me, and behind Bruce. I think when they finally saw all that — no matter what they did, NBC was not going to allow them to take over this whole situation — I think they said, 'To heck with it. Everybody go home.'"

Thus in 1976 one of the most serious problems in the history of National Bank of Commerce was ended. The Memphis directors, with the assistance of attorney Bill Izlar, reached an agreement in principal with the rest of the UTBC board in which Nashville City Bank and Trust Company and First Trust and Savings Bank, Paris, would be divested and would no longer remain subsidiaries of United Tennessee Bancshares Corporation effective January 1, 1977. Therefore, as the sole remaining subsidiary of UTBC, National Bank of Commerce was returned

While from a financial perspective the construction of Commerce Square tied up a large amount of capital, the building provided the bank a landmark. Today the presence of National Bank of Commerce towers over the Memphis city skyline.

to Memphis management and ownership. At the same time, the directors agreed that the bank and holding company boards would be identical. For more than a year the bank continued to operate under the UTBC name until April 1978, when United Tennessee Bancshares Corporation changed its name to National Commerce Bancorporation to more closely identify with its sole banking subsidiary, National Bank of Commerce.

With the bank and its holding company united under its own directors, the institution was able again to direct its entire attention to what had always been its primary activity — the business of banking. Effective management and modernized operations quickly produced results. On April 7, 1977, Bruce Campbell announced that the bank's total deposits had reached $420 million. At the end of 1981 the bank's deposits had grown to $547 million while total assets had increased to $743 million.

Impressive though this growth was, it was limited by a major problem remaining from the previous era: The bank's 32-story tower which had been completed in 1972. In 1977, the bank owned 60 percent of this office building. Described as a "drag" on the earnings of the bank, it had achieved an occupancy rate of only about 72 percent. But merely increasing the tower's occupancy would not solve the problem, which was the amount of capital tied up in the building and producing insufficient returns.

In an interview for *The Commercial Appeal* on April 7, 1977, Campbell said, "We've made a $10 million initial investment in that building, and we are paying a monthly lease fee. But under the agreement with the insurance company that owns the other 40 percent of the building, we haven't received any income from the building, and we really don't expect to for another two years."

The problem, which became apparent to the officers and directors, was not in the quality of the building; instead, it was in the amount of capital that was tied up in its ownership. Wayne Pyeatt later said, "Really, honestly, we probably, at that time at least, ought not to have built that building. That was not a very wise move. We were a comparatively small bank, and we did not need to have that kind of investment... The building did two things. It gave us great stature, I guess, in Memphis, and, on the other hand, it was really a problem with regard to earnings. The bank never lost money on the building, we just didn't make as much money." In spite of the financial difficulty, the bank's leaders recognized the symbolic value of the new bank building. W. Neely Mallory had the following observation: "A magnificent building...I think it is a very handsome tower. My recall is that some of the financial problems involved with the tower were certainly equal to its beauty."

The need to sell the tower was obvious for several years, but the size and value of it made finding a buyer difficult. By the mid-1980s conditions became favorable for a sale. As W. Neely Mallory noted, "In the roaring Eighties, the big stock brokerage firms were putting together real estate syndicates, and the tax laws made those kinds of investments look attractive."

Bruce Campbell's recollection of the sale was that: "We would have made the decision anytime we thought we could have gotten out, but in 1984 there was a good deal of building activity in downtown Memphis. The limited partnerships were very popular, and so there were a lot of real estate deals. We engaged Goldman Sachs to tell us what sort of value the property had. We were fully leased and making money in the building at that point, but nothing like what we could make if we freed up that capital. Goldman did not buy it. It was bought by an E. F. Hutton syndicate off the West Coast. Goldman was the agent we used to consummate the deal."

The timing of the sale was excellent. The fluctuations of the economy, and real estate in particular, had been downward both before and after this period, but the sale was negotiated at a favorable period in the cycle. Robert G. Snowden, a professional realtor with a lifetime of experience, said, "We were very, very fortunate. We made the switch at the right moment in time. I don't know how we did it. I honestly don't." W. Neely Mallory said, "What turned the real estate economy down as much as anything were the tax laws made passive losses no longer deductible. I would say we were both wise and lucky at the time we picked to dispose of it."

Disposing of the tower at favorable terms thus solved the second problem inherited by the Bruce Campbell administration. The terms negotiated at the sale included keeping the corporate logo at the top of the tower and a lease that extended into the 21st century for needed space in the building. Because of the boom in real estate investment of the time, the building was sold profitably. John D. Canale said afterward: "At one time, we thought it might be a good deal to sell the whole damn thing for $14 million. Fortunately, we didn't. . .It sold for $46 million." Approximately 71 percent of this total went to the bank.

The positive results of the sale were experienced quickly. Bruce Campbell commented that, although getting into the construction of the tower might have seemed to be a good idea at the time, "getting out of it was a better idea...Look at the operating figures prior to that time and since that time — it's a real stairstep in the operating performance. It allowed, for the first time, the good things that were going on financially in the company to show through in our operating results. They had been masked by the weight of that tower." Another bank officer said, "We got a very good price for the building and were able to get a huge capital gain on the sale. And we were able to take some of those profits and plow them into our reserves which had been, I think, somewhat weak in terms of its provisions. And we were able to get ahead a little bit on our reserving; most importantly, we got rid of an under-performing asset."

Difficulties associated with the UTBC holding company and the tower were the two greatest problems of the Bruce Campbell era. And the successful solutions of handicaps were significant accomplishments of the time. Just as the victory in the holding company struggle won independence for National Bank of Commerce, the favorable sale of the tower provided a large amount of capital needed to expand banking operations and profitability. A publication by the bank in June 1987 noted that the growth of the bank was again underway. It stated, "NBC proved itself to be the premier commercial bank in Memphis, handling the majority of middle and upper corporate clients in the area."

During this period, the bank had exceptionally professional management from its chief executive officer, but such remarkable growth required the trained talents of an entire staff. Campbell's account is as follows: "Shortly after I came to NBC, the key group that had been making main office loans for the company was gone, either through death or retirement...We had a key decision to make. We had some young, green, untrained, unseasoned people on board, and we could take them and go with them — they were by and large Memphis or Memphis area natives — as the future management of the bank, or we would have to go out and interview and hire in through some head hunters people to staff the bank. It was my strong feeling that because of the long-term advantage the bank would have by having home-grown, home-trained people, and, while it was going to be rough in the early stages, it would pay big dividends down the road for us to go with the younger crowd and just weather the period when they were green. If we could get through that the best we could, we would be better off in the long run...The cadre of managers I am referring to is still with the company in various senior capacities...It was the right decision, a good decision, and has paid off."

Effective team work is required for banking suc-

cess, for even a great leader cannot succeed without an equivalent degree of support from many others who must also serve a large institution. It is not enough merely to recruit and train employees. They must also be inspired and motivated to exceptional performance. When Bruce Campbell arrived at National Bank of Commerce, its salary levels were quite low. Improving this situation became a leading priority.

By 1993, he was able to describe this progress at the bank as follows: "If you look at the standards on a per head basis, we would be just about the highest, if not the highest, in the South in terms of what we pay our people. We have been at it for 24 years, but it is not so much base pay. We are really strong believers in incentive pay. We have incentive pay at every level in the company. For work done there is a monetary benefit. If employees exceed the norm, they get paid. So we monitor it, we set it up, and we focus our people with financial rewards. Since early on we have been using incentives much more than a lot of banking companies. Given the youth of our staff, it has been a real motivator for them. We have, I would say, reasonable base salaries, but our base salaries would not necessarily compare that favorably with others'. But, when you add together the base pay plus the incentive pay, we are ahead of almost anybody else...We have had since 1978 an employee stock ownership plan. The bank makes an unmatched contribution to this every year for the benefit of our employees."

With capable and highly motivated leadership at all levels, the institution was able to move aggressively into its major activity: Increasing its volume of successful loans that would produce profits for its stockholders. An important part of the bank's success in lending during this era was a result of things it did not do. Generally, it did not make bad loans. The credit files were brought up to date and kept current. The greatest attention to lending situations was made at the beginning of transactions. Bruce Campbell's explanation was: "One thing we have going — we make good loan decisions at the front door. A bum loan decision is a real weight to the company because of the man-hours it ties up. So, the best decision is made on the front end by whether or not to go into the loan."

The success of this careful lending policy was noted by W. Neely Mallory, who said: "I would hate to name names or stories, but there are some people — seemingly big, rich people — who came in and said, 'I want to make a million dollar loan.' And the bank would say that was fine, 'we will be happy to lend you a million dollars, just sign your name on the note right here.' The customer said, 'Well look, I don't ever sign things personally.' The bank replied, 'then we won't do any business with you.'"

During this period, many other banks became heavily involved in making foreign loans, and some incurred substantial losses from them. National Bank of Commerce scrupulously avoided participating in this trend. Robert G. Snowden remarked, "We have not done that...Foreign lending to us is a couple of hundred miles away." John D. Canale, Jr. said, "We didn't have any foreign loans...We don't want to be where we can't keep track of it to find out just what is going on."

It was to the credit of the bank also that it wisely avoided involvement in real estate investment trusts (REITs) during this era. Bruce Campbell's account was: "A lot of money was going into REITs during that period, and we were fortunate in missing that industry totally. We stayed away from them. We could never get comfortable with this industry and the way it was running — not to say there were not some good ones out there, but we didn't believe we were smart enough to pick them, so we stayed away from the industry, and it saved us a lot of grief during that period."

By following these policies, National Bank of Commerce increased its lending with an unusual degree of profitability because of the low amount of investment capital lost in bad loans. Bruce Campbell's analysis was: "You take what cards you have and you deal with those. We did have some strengths in our young and increasingly seasoned group of commercial lenders. So we focused there, put our energy there, put

our key people there and had some successes in the late Seventies and up into the Eighties." This strategy was effective and the bank grew steadily during these years. By 1983, the total assets of National Bank of Commerce had reached $1 billion.

There are two ways to measure the effectiveness of the leadership of the bank during the Bruce Campbell era. One is by the record of growth and profitability of the company, and the other is by the evaluations of those familiar with the institution and its leader.

Several individuals who were present as observers and participants in the history of the bank during the recent decades have provided their evaluations. There is a remarkable uniformity in their views. Benjamin Goodman, who has been associated with the bank longer than most of its current employees have lived, said, "I think you have the best CEO that I know right now — Mr. Campbell. He has an understanding of people. He isn't the military kind of bureaucrat. He is sensitive, and, I think, he is very skillful in his knowledge of the intricacies of the banking business, which people really don't understand. He surrounds himself with good executives, he gives them responsibility, and he expects results, but he doesn't tell them exactly what to do."

Walter P. Armstrong, Jr., a director emeritus, noted: "I would say that Bruce's greatest contribution was the reorganization of the administration of the bank. He brought excellent people into key positions. He tightened the organization, he cut down on the personnel and made it more effective...he greatly increased the efficiency of the bank. He also brought in a number of major customers and clients of the bank, and he kept a very tight rein on how things operated."

Lucius E. Burch, Jr., a director emeritus who was involved with the bank when Campbell arrived, said: "The bank has been going in the right way ever since he arrived. Bruce's experience had been — he was doing what John Evans (senior loan officer) has been doing on the credit side — he came in and expanded greatly and very quickly in his managerial skill and his recognition of industry problems."

Rudi E. Scheidt, a director active in the management of the bank, credited Bruce Campbell's practice of, "solid, conservative banking. He is a bankers' banker who avoids mistakes and keeps things from flying too high. He made a great contribution by bringing in young leadership, such as Tom Garrott."

John D. Canale, Jr., a director emeritus whose family has historically been associated with the bank, spoke of the strengths Bruce Campbell brought: "The best that I know of was his judgment, and particularly strength in loans. That is what he was doing in Atlanta, where he came from. He had a pretty deep background in banking...He taught all of these men who are the mainstays there now — like John Evans and the younger men, too — all of them. That's where they really got their banking experience."

Robert G. Snowden, also a director emeritus whose family has been associated with the bank for more than a century, provided his perspective: "Bruce is probably the best banker in this part of the country, but the least understood or appreciated by the public, because he does not seek any publicity...He is a banker, very first class, and you can rely on what he says and thinks...He was head of the lending department. Of course, he was one of the first people I dealt with because we were borrowing pretty good sums of money, and he was responsible to see that we didn't walk off with the bank. He put restraints on us and everybody else that he needed to, and I respected him completely. He brought Tom Garrott into the bank because he needed to get a successor, and he thought he needed to get somebody strong from the outside." Concerning the present status of the bank's management, Snowden said, "I would say it is absolutely at its peak. If I had to pick a year since I have known anything about it, I would say it is at its peak."

W. Neely Mallory, another director whose family has an association with the bank extending over several generations, analyzed the current administration of the bank as follows: "Bruce is probably as good as they

come...He put the bank in order. He built the loan loss reserves. He concentrated on making quality loans as opposed to making loans. He knows how to leverage the capital of the bank. He knows how to balance the assets and the liabilities...He is just a brilliant banker. He has gathered around him some quiet, smart, hard working, effective people, and he has a bank that I think is the envy of the banks in the Southeast if not in the country...I see NBC's team viewing its job as how to make maximum return on its assets and, certainly I mean that in the context of doing it in a prudent and safe way...I think there is a difference in saying, 'I am a banker,' than, 'I am a steward for the stockholders to see how I can take the assets we have gathered and earn more for the stockholders.' It just sets them apart...The most important thing, I think, for the chief executive officer is to run a good operation and develop plans and strategies to enhance the value of the stockholders' investment. I don't see NBC today with any concerted effort to grab the headlines. It is grabbing a lot of headlines because it is a well run bank. So I think if we want to get into the headlines, we are better off running a damn good bank than we are having the president of the bank as president of the united fund."

Wayne W. Pyeatt, who worked with many members of the present management team of the bank, evaluated the current era of leadership from the perspective of his experience: "Bruce brought something to the bank that we needed very badly. He brought a certain expertise with regard to lending because he had been in a big bank. He brought a way of operating, a total lending effort...He also brought a certain kind of meticulous thinking. He is a very meticulous person who does not jump. Bruce thinks before he does anything, and he will think something all the way through. He has wonderful judgment, not only about lending. He has wonderful judgment about situations and he looks very well at the future...Bruce trained most of his people...He was never one to put himself forward in the community...Bruce loves that bank, and he loves to watch it grow and prosper. And, he loves those people around him. He has a very loyal cadre of folks there, and I admire him immensely for being able to do that."

The truest measure of the success of any financial institution, however, is not in the evaluations of others, however authoritative and informed they may be. The real standard of success for a bank is how successfully it can expand its income producing operations. For National Bank of Commerce, the greatest breakthrough into increased profitability took place during the decade of the 1980s, and it was in a new area of major operations for the institution — retail banking. Although Campbell credits it to the effectiveness of the entire management team of the bank, it was the result of a brilliantly innovative concept developed by a new officer, Thomas M. Garrott.

A native of Mississippi, Garrott was educated at Baylor School in Chattanooga, and attended Vanderbilt University where he graduated with a B.A. degree in economics. After serving two years as an officer in the United States Navy, he entered the Wharton School of the University of Pennsylvania from which he graduated in 1962 with a M.B.A. degree in finance and banking. He moved to Memphis, married Allison Moore from Charlotte, North Carolina, and achieved rapid success with Malone and Hyde, Inc., then the third largest food wholesaler in the nation. He was promoted to the position of executive vice president for finance and admin-

Thomas McMurry Garrott

istration. His duties at Malone and Hyde led to his appointment to the Board of Directors of National Bank of Commerce, which led to his association with Bruce Campbell.

In 1982, a momentous event in the history of the bank took place: Bruce Campbell invited Thomas Garrott to come down to the company and have a cup of coffee. At this meeting, Campbell offered Garrott the position of president of both the bank and its holding company. At first, Garrott was not interested, for he had given consideration to going into business for himself. After several weeks of deliberation and discussion with his wife, his recollection is that: "Ultimately we came to the decision that I would take the opportunity and give it a five year commitment...Bruce and I, after several weeks of discussion, laid out an agenda of what our various responsibilities would be, the things he would like for me to focus on, and one of the areas was the retail side of the bank. This bank had long been known for its credit quality and its importance in the commercial lending area, but we had missed the opportunity of retail because our two principal competitors, First Tennessee and Union Planters, had built vast networks right after World War II, and this bank was a distant third in moving into retail market development."

Garrott's success in meeting this challenge followed rapidly. His explanation was: "There are a lot of similarities in the banking business and the grocery business, and I think actually the grocery business prepared me very well for the banking business in that both businesses are very high-volume, transaction-oriented businesses where the velocity and turnover are really more important than the margin. In a lot of businesses, business people are thinking about their gross margin, or in the case of a bank, their net interest margin, and one can lose sight of the fact that you are in a very thin margin business where velocity and turnover are actually more important than the margin. Retailers learned that years ago, drove their prices down, increased their market share, and ran the competitors out of business. Banks have been slow to catch on in that regard. Money, being a commodity, has made it especially difficult for banks to differentiate one from another. It is fungible and difficult to gain an advantage over your competitors. The same principles about velocity and turnover apply, however, and that is the concept which we brought to the bank that led us into retail banking in a significant way."

As president of the bank, Garrott focused successfully on operational improvements, including reducing the operating expenses of the institution and divesting it of the unproductive office tower. But he continued to focus also on the basic problem of developing the retail area of business. The bank's operations had already achieved exceptional efficiency and the commercial lending activity could hardly be made more successful, so great were the advances that had been made.

New branch banks had been established, but further opportunities to open additional ones were limited and the expense of building these facilities was high. At that time, the cost of acquiring land and opening a new branch was in the range of $500,000 to $700,000. Even with the capital available from the sale of the bank's tower, substantial expansion in this area would be difficult and limited at best.

The solution that Garrott developed for this problem, with the approval of Bruce Campbell and the support of the entire management team of the bank, was

revolutionary. And it had not previously been done successfully by bankers anywhere in the nation. Other banks had attempted to organize similar operations in at least two other cities, but had not been able to implement them successfully.

Because of his successful background in both the grocery business and banking, Garrott was able to ask himself a question that challenged assumptions formerly considered fundamental in the banking industry: Was it even necessary for financial institutions to construct branch facilities in order to expand their retail banking operations?

The answer was that this expensive expansion was not necessary, provided that other satisfactory locations could be found. He found such locations, for they already existed, in the immense grocery supermarkets that had grown up in all urban locations during the past few decades. These capacious buildings, strategically placed by grocery firms at sites convenient to the buying population of the nation's cities and towns, were patronized on a regular basis by great numbers of people. Why could banking services not also be offered at these excellent locations?

Thus the concept took form. It was the most important new initiative in the history of National Bank of Commerce and one of the truly unique developments in the history of American banking. But the idea still had to be successfully implemented. Fortunately, the bank had two major assets in the undertaking. One was a long-standing, cooperative association with the Kroger Company which had endured for many years. The Kroger Company had been one of the loyal corporate friends whose support had helped save the bank from loss in the financial crisis during the Great Depression. The other major asset was its president, Thomas Garrott, who, because of his past experience, had extensive contacts among leaders in the grocery business.

In 1985, the alliance between National Bank of Commerce and the Kroger Company was formed. Utilizing building space already available, it arranged

The advantage that supermarket banking provides customers is the convenience of one-stop shopping. National Bank of Commerce's first supermarket branch was opened in the Kroger supermarket on Exeter Road in Germantown, a Memphis suburb, in September 1985.

for branches of the bank to be opened inside Kroger supermarkets. The arrangement was of great benefit to customers who needed to do both banking and grocery shopping. A substantial savings in cost was involved, for it was possible to open a facility in a supermarket for about one tenth of the cost of constructing a new branch. And the presence of customers was assured, because everyone found it necessary to purchase food.

Details of the new arrangement were implemented by September 1985. In that month, the first of these full-service facilities was opened and a Kroger official joined the Boards of Directors of National Commerce Bancorporation and its subsidiary, National Bank of Commerce. He was James A. LeRoy, vice president of the Delta Marketing Area of Kroger.

The first of the new banking centers, called Money Market branches but later to be designated Super Money Market® branches, was opened in the Kroger store on Exeter Road in Germantown, a Memphis sub-

urb. The grand opening celebration was held on September 11, 1985. This new kind of branch proved to be so successful that others were soon being opened throughout the Memphis area.

Moving quickly to take advantage of the unprecedented opportunities, National Commerce Bancorporation formed two bank subsidiaries in other Tennessee cities. The first of these state chartered institutions was Nashville Bank of Commerce, organized in 1985. The following year, NBC Knoxville Bank was established. Within five years, the Knoxville bank was operating eight Super Money Market® branches and the Nashville bank had 14. These were so successful that there had been no need to construct any of the expensive, traditional banking facilities.

By 1992, National Commerce Bancorporation operated 39 Super Money Market® branches, and their success was recognized throughout the nation. In the meantime, NCBC had formed a supermarket banking affiliate, National Commerce Bank Services, Inc., with Douglas W. Ferris, Jr. as president, to license this concept to other banks on a nationwide basis. By the end of the year, NCBC had assisted 73 banking companies, operating 213 supermarket branches nationwide.

With its capital freed for banking use by the sale of the tower and its retail operations expanded by the Kroger alliance, National Bank of Commerce entered a period of growth in the mid-1980s that has continued through the remaining years of the Bruce Campbell era. According to an article in the magazine, *Bank Management* in August 1991, the number of the bank's retail customers had increased during the past decade from 30,000 to 140,000, a phenomenal percentage of increase for any financial institution. Further favorable information was reported in the article: "Led by the growth of its company-owned Super Money Market in-store branch network as well as its branch licensing operations, NCBC has diversified to the point that its wholesale/retail mix is now 50/50, a sharp change from 10 years ago when the bulk of its business was wholesale."

The consistently outstanding performance of National Commerce Bancorporation had not gone unnoticed by members of the financial community, both regional and national. In 1992, the highly regard-

National Commerce Bancorporation formed two bank subsidiaries operating solely through supermarket branches, Nashville Bank of Commerce (1985) and NBC Knoxville Bank (1986). Within five years, the Knoxville bank was operating eight supermarket locations and the Nashville bank, 14.

ed rating agency, Thomson BankWatch, Inc., that exclusively monitors financial institutions, raised its rating for NCBC's overall quality to "A" from "A/B." This rating was the highest given by the agency, whose analysts follow more than 500 financial companies.

National Commerce Bancorporation received additional recognition in 1992. In a survey of 144 of the nation's largest bank holding companies, financial industry investment specialists Keefe, Bruyette & Woods, Inc. ranked NCBC second in compound growth in earnings per share, placing it among the elite group of only eight bank holding companies in the survey that had suffered no year-to-year declines in earnings per share since 1980. This marked NCBC's fifth consecutive year to be named to KBW's prestigious "Honor Roll."

The year 1993 was destined to be a significant one in the history of the 120-year old National Bank of Commerce. It began with its parent company, National Commerce Bancorporation (NCBC) having grown to $2.3 billion in assets. And its continued efforts to achieve the greatest possible effectiveness in its operations had been remarkably successful. According to information produced by Thomson BankWatch, Inc., NCBC had led all major bank holding companies in the Southeast in its efficiency ratio during 1991, with an efficiency

The company's officers (seated from left) are Bruce E. Campbell, Jr., chairman of the board; Thomas M. Garrott, president; (standing from left) John S. Evans, vice chairman and senior loan officer; William R. Reed, Jr., vice chairman; and Walter B. Howell, Jr., vice chairman and chief financial officer.

ratio of 54.90 percent. That is, it cost the firm $54.90 to produce $100.00 in income. The two leading local competitors of NCBC had efficiency ratios of 67.02 percent and 68.67 percent. The efficiency ratios for 1992, which had just become available, brought the good news that NCBC had improved its ratio to 54.10 percent. The beginning of 1993 also brought the news that National Bank of Commerce's deposit total for Memphis had passed that of Union Planters National Bank so it thus ranked second behind First Tennessee Bank in Memphis-area marketshare.

On February 11, 1993, members of the National Bank of Commerce community officially learned how important the year would be in the history of their institution. The following press release was made public: "Bruce E. Campbell, Chairman of the Board and Chief Executive Officer of National Commerce Bancorporation (NCBC) and its lead bank, National Bank of Commerce (NBC), Memphis, Tennessee, today announced that he plans to relinquish those positions on May 1, 1993. Thomas M. Garrott, 55, President of both NCBC and NBC, will become Chairman, President and Chief Executive Officer of NCBC, as well as Chairman and CEO of NBC. John S. Evans, 53, Vice Chairman and Senior Loan Officer of NBC, will become President of National Bank of Commerce."

Information compiled by Walter B. Howell, Jr., vice chairman and chief financial officer of the bank, summarized the accomplishment of the administration that was coming to a close: "Since 1977, when Campbell became CEO, NCBC has had 15 years of consecutive double-digit percentage increases in net income. Assets have grown from $589 million to $2.3 billion, while net income has risen from $2.9 million to $34 million. Return on average assets was 0.5 percent in 1977 compared to 1.6 percent in 1992, while return on equity was 9.6 percent in 1977 compared to 18.8 percent in 1992. Over the 15-year period, the average annual increase in earnings per share was approximately 17 percent, while dividends grew at an average

annual rate of 17 percent. The price of the company's stock rose from $1.26 (adjusted for all stock dividends and splits) at year-end 1977 to $29.00 on January 31, 1993, for an average annual increase of 23 percent. At year-end 1992, the company's stockholder equity was $199 million or 8.7 percent of year-end assets."

Campbell, who had been working for two years with a management transition committee of the Board of Directors in preparation for the change, announced to his employees: "I have great confidence in Tom Garrott to lead the company and in John Evans and the other company managers not only to continue but to enhance the company's performance in the years ahead. I am proud of the staff and what they have been able to accomplish for our common good during my years as CEO. This is an appropriate time for such a change. The company has just completed an excellent year, is in a very strong financial condition, is in an attractive competitive situation, and is fortunate in having a cadre of senior managers who are seasoned and tested. Although less active, I will remain keenly interested in the company's progress and will be assisting the new management team whenever possible."

Campbell agreed to continue as chairman of the executive committee of both the corporation and its lead bank, and to continue to serve on the Boards of Directors of NCBC and National Bank of Commerce. As on most occasions in the past, the bank's tradition of stability and continuity of leadership was assured.

Thus with the passage of leadership from Bruce E. Campbell, Jr. to Thomas M. Garrott on May 1, 1993, one era in the history of National Bank of Commerce comes to an end and another begins. And the responsibility of directing the course of the institution passes from its 12th to its 13th president. For 120 years it has shared the successes and the disasters of the area it serves, Memphis and the Mid-South. It has passed through six of its nation's wars, as well as various depressions, recessions, and times of boom and prosperity. It has survived panics, hard times, a run by its depositors, and an attempted takeover by outsiders.

Institutions are like human beings in that they are formed by their history — that is, by the various experiences they have during their existence. And Lucius Burch is correct in his observation that, "Banks do have characteristics of their own, and NBC has some that have existed for many years." The distinctive nature of National Bank of Commerce has been shaped by the events, recounted in the previous pages, that have occurred through the century and one-fifth of its existence.

This is a long time indeed. It is longer than the span of a human life and longer also than that of most financial institutions. But throughout its entire history, this bank has experienced an unusual continuity with the individuals who have been associated with it. Many of its stockholders, directors, and employees have maintained their connection with it for an exceptionally long time. Further, a sizable number of relationships with the bank have been continued by successive generations of the same families. In this sense, 120 years has produced less change in the character of the institution, simply because there has been so much continuity among the people involved.

This may be noted in the fact that the entire history of the bank has been shared by two individuals.

Nineteen-twenty-seven was an important date in the institution's history because it was the time the association of one man with the bank ended and that of another one began. In 1927, the Bank of Commerce and Trust Company lost the services of one of its directors, Oliver Hazard Perry Piper, a Civil War veteran who was the last surviving member of the group of founders who had established the bank in 1873. Shortly before Piper's death at the age of 89, a young attorney who had just graduated from Harvard University Law School returned to Memphis to join the Wilson, Gates and Armstrong law firm that was associated with the bank. Today, this attorney, Benjamin Goodman, now almost 90 years of age, still has vivid memories of his long association with the bank. Thus the lives of two individuals have spanned the complete 120-year history of National Bank of Commerce.

The greatest influence in forming the character of the bank has always been the quality of the people who served it. They kept it open every business day since it began operations on April 1, 1873. And it is the character and fidelity of those who now serve the institution that will guide it through the next era of its history. As John D. Canale said, "The bank is built on concrete and not on sand."

.

EPILOGUE

TODAY'S
NATIONAL BANK OF COMMERCE

At this writing, National Bank of Commerce, with 29 branch locations, is the lead bank of National Commerce Bancorporation, a $2.3 billion financial institution headquartered in Memphis, Tennessee. NCBC's additional banking subsidiaries are Nashville Bank of Commerce and NBC Knoxville Bank operating 16 and 10 branches, respectively.

In addition to traditional banking services, the company offers investment advice through Commerce Capital Management, Inc., investment services through Commerce Investment Corporation, data processing capabilities through Commerce General Corporation, consumer credit through Commerce Finance Company, and supermarket banking to licensed banks through National Commerce Bank Services, Inc.

Shortly after the completion of this text, National Commerce Bancorporation Chairman of the Board Bruce E. Campbell, Jr. received word that the company had reached another milestone.

Stating "consistency is rewarded," financial industry investment specialists Keefe, Bruyette & Woods, Inc. named NCBC first in the nation for compound growth in earnings per share. The ranking, announced April 16, places NCBC in an elite group of only eight bank holding companies, of 144 institutions surveyed, to have suffered no year-to-year declines in earnings per share since 1980. The year 1993 marks NCBC's sixth consecutive year to be named to KBW's prestigious "Honor Roll."

TERMS OF LEADERSHIP

NATIONAL BANK OF COMMERCE
CHIEF EXECUTIVES, YEARS SERVED

Edgar McDavitt 1873-1874

John T. Fargason 1874-1880

Samuel H. Dunscomb 1880-1898

John T. Fargason 1898-1909

Oliver H. P. Piper 1909-1910

Thomas O. Vinton.......................................1910-1933

William R. King...1933-1940

Richard B. Barton..1940-1948

William B. Pollard 1948-1957

James L. Ross...1957-1965

Lewis K. McKee...1965-1974

Wayne W. Pyeatt 1974-1976

Bruce E. Campbell, Jr. 1976-1993

Thomas M. Garrott 1993-

ROSTER OF DIRECTORS

NATIONAL BANK OF COMMERCE AND NATIONAL COMMERCE BANCORPORATION DIRECTORS SINCE 1873

Note: The individual's affiliation is as of his election to the board.

Nathan Adams...................Life Association of America

Thomas H. Allen...............................Cotton Merchant

S. B. Anderson......................Anderson-Tully Company

O. C. Armstrong...............................William R. Moore
Dry Goods Company

Walter P. Armstrong, Jr. ....Armstrong, Allen,
Braden, Goodman, McBride & Prewitt

Frank G. Barton ....F. G. Barton Cotton Company

Frank G. Barton, Jr. ....Barton Equipment Company

R. B. Barton ....F. G. Barton Cotton Company

B. Bayliss ....B. Bayliss & Company - Cotton

B. B. Beecher......................................Cotton Merchant

Albert W. Biggs...Attorney

M. S. Binswanger ....Binswanger & Company

Jack R. Blair.......................................Smith & Nephew
Surgical Products Group

Hugh M. Brinkley..............Planter - Hughes, Arkansas

R. Grattan Brown, Jr................Montedonico, Heiskell,
Davis, Glankler, Brown & Gilliland
Attorneys at Law

Lucius E. Burch, Jr. ....Burch, Porter &
Johnson, Attorneys at Law

Bruce E. Campbell, Jr. .....National Bank of Commerce

John Canale ....D. Canale Company

John D. Canale, Jr. ....D. Canale & Company

John D. Canale, III ....D. Canale Food Services, Inc.

Phil M. Canale.......................Canale, Glankler, Little,
Boone & Loch

Edmond D. Cicala ....Goldsmith's Department Store

R. L. Cochran......E. L. Cochran & Company - Lumber

Fred Collins ....Bank of Commerce & Trust Company

Russell T. Cramer ....United Tennessee
Bancshares Corporation

J. S. Day.....Day, Horton & Bailey - Wholesale Grocers

John W. Dillard ......Dillard & Coffin - Cotton Products

Paul Dillard ....Dillard & Coffin Company
Cotton Products

James K. Dobbs, III ....Dobbs Management Service

Donald Drinkard.....................William R. Moore, Inc.

W. B. Dunavant, Jr............Dunavant Enterprises, Inc.

S. H. Dunscomb ....DeSoto Insurance Company

J. M. Edwards ....LNO&T Railroad

James Elder ....Banker

J. A. Evans................Farnsworth - Evans & Company

John S. Evans...................National Bank of Commerce

John W. Falls ....Real Estate

J. T. Fargason ....J. T. Fargason Company

J. T. Fargason, Jr.................J. T. Fargason & Company
Wholesale Grocers

Thomas C. Farnsworth, Jr. ....The Crow-Farnsworth
Companies

William W. Fischer................................Fischer Lime &
Cement Company

John T. Fisher.............John T. Fisher Motor Company

John H. Fizer ....Estes, Fizer & Company - Cotton

Roy Flowers ....Planter - Mattson, Mississippi

D. W. Fly ....Fly & Hobson Company

Frederick Fowler ....Bank of Commerce &
Trust Company

Godfrey Frank...................Godfrey Frank & Company

Thomas M. Garrott ....Malone & Hyde
Financial Corporation

M. Gavin....M. Gavin & Company - Wholesale Grocers

Frank J. Glankler....................Canale, Glankler, Little,
Boone & Loch

E. J. Goldsmith..............J. Goldsmith & Sons Company

E. J. Goldsmith, Jr........J. Goldsmith & Sons Company

A. B. Goodbar........Goodbar, Love & Company - Shoes

J. B. Goodbar ....Goodbar Shoe Company

J. W. Goodbar..........................Goodbar Shoe Company

Abe Goodman..Capitalist

Charles F. Goodman ......American Finishing Company

Paul T. Graves ....Pure Oil Company

A. D. Gwynne ....Stewart Gwynne Company

C. J. Haase ....Marx and Bensdorf, Inc.

Henry H. Haizlip.................Porter - Weaver Company

Henry Halle ....Henry Halle & Bro.

J. T. Harahan...........................IC Railroad Company
Chicago, Illinois

Julien J. Hohenberg......Hohenberg Brothers Company

George S. Hooper..............George S. Hooper Company

Walter B. Howell, Jr........National Bank of Commerce

H. E. Jackson ....Estes & Jackson, Attorneys

R. Lee Jenkins...............Schering - Plough Corporation
and Plough Inc.

Fred B. Jones..............................Perkins Oil Company

Thomas M. Keesee ....John Wellford Company

W. R. King.....William R. Moore Dry Goods Company

William D. Kyser...Attorney

James A. LeRoy ....The Kroger Company

Leo J. Levy.......................................Julius Levy & Sons

W. E. Love..............Wynn - Love & Company - Cotton

E. Lowenstein............................B. Lowenstein & Bros.

Fred W. Lucas ....Allenberg Cotton Company

G. W. MacRae..Banker

J. E. McCadden....................Armstrong - McCadden,
Allen, Braden & Goodman

E. McDavitt ....Bank of Commerce

S. F. McDonald ....McDonald & Prest

Michael McDonnell.................The Jordan Companies

James E. McGehee, Jr..................James E. McGehee &
Company, Inc.

Lewis K. McKee...............National Bank of Commerce

Eugene Magevney..Educator

W. B. Mallory ....W. B. Mallory & Sons Company

W. M. Mallory ....W. B. Mallory & Sons Company

W. Neely Mallory...........Memphis Compress & Storage
Company

W. Neely Mallory, Jr..............................Mallory Farms
Chatfield, Arkansas

W. W. Mallory.............W. B. Mallory & Sons Company

S. Mansfield ....S. Mansfield & Company - Drugs

H. H. Maury ....Webb & Maury - Grain

John S. Montedonico...............Canale, Glankler, Little,
Boone & Loch

J. V. Montedonico.............National Bank of Commerce

John W. Montesi.................Liberty Cash Grocers, Inc.

Russell E. Mooney............National Bank of Commerce

H. Morris...Banker

H. C. Nall.................Nall, Williams Tobacco Company
Louisville, Kentucky

James Nathan...Banker

F. M. Nelson ....Insurance

J. P. Norfleet..Sledge & Norfleet

R. Vance Norfleet ....Sledge & Norfleet

W. L. Oates ....McFadden & Oates

J. A. Omberg ....National Bank of Commerce

Joseph Orgill, Jr. ....Orgill Brothers & Company

Max B. Ostner, Sr. ....James E. McGehee &
Company, Inc.

John Overton, Jr. ....Overton & Overton - Real Estate

S. Watkins Overton ....Mayor, City of Memphis

C. W. Parham............C. W. Parham Lumber Company

A. L. Parker....................................The Peabody Hotel

Harry J. Phillips, Sr. ...Browning - Ferris Industries, Inc.

William G. Phillips......................Goodlett & Company

O. H. P. Piper..Capitalist

W. B. Pollard....................National Bank of Commerce

R. R. Prest ....McDonald & Prest

Bem Price ....Oxford, Mississippi

A. L. Pritchard.................................Pritchard Brothers

William Pritchard ....Lumber

Wayne W. Pyeatt ....National Bank of Commerce

W. A. Ramson.......................Gayoso Lumber Company

George Randolph...Attorney

William R. Reed, Jr...........National Bank of Commerce

E. L. Rice...........Bank of Commerce & Trust Company

J. L. Ross...........................National Bank of Commerce

W. H. Russe ....Russe & Burgess Lumber Company

C. R. Ryan ....Wholesale Grocery

Rudi E. Scheidt............Hohenberg Brothers Company

Erich L. Schmied.........S. & W. Construction Company

Henry C. Self.............................Planter & Industrialist

Marks, Mississippi

J. W. Shepherd.................................Shepherd Brothers

Cleland K. Smith...............................Cotton Merchant

R. Bogardus Snowden ....Capitalist

R. Brinkley Snowden ....Bank of Commerce &

Trust Company

R. Brinkley Snowden, Jr. ...Planter - Hughes, Arkansas

Robert G. Snowden ....Wilkinson & Snowden

Robert M. Solmson ....RFS, Inc.

R. A. Speed...Grain Dealer

David Sternberg.................Sternberg & Sons - Tobacco

Leon Sternberger ....Sternberger - McKee Company

Sidney A. Stewart, Jr........The Crump Companies, Inc.

J. Sugarman...Insurance

James A. Sweeney ....National Bank of Commerce

J. A. Taylor.......................Taylor & Carroll - Attorneys

R. A. Taylor ......DeSoto Hardwood Flooring Company

R. Lee Taylor ....Private Investor

W. F. Taylor...Cotton Factor

L. A. Thornton.................National Bank of Commerce

T. B. Trezevant..........Gorsuch & Trezevant-Merchants

W. G. Thomas ....Pidgeon-Thomas Iron Works

T. B. Turley...Attorney

T. H. Tutwiler........Memphis Street Railway Company

T. O. Vinton.......Bank of Commerce & Trust Company

McKay Van Vleet ....Van Vleet-Mansfield

Drug Company

P. P. Van Vleet.....Van Vleet-Mansfield Drug Company

Robert P. Walters ....Fischer Lime & Cement Company

William S. Walters...Fischer Lime & Cement Company

William S. Walters, Jr............................Fischer Lime &

Cement Company

John H. Watkins...Bank of Commerce & Trust Company

H. Wetter ....Wetter Manufacturing Company

W. N. Wilkerson...........................IMC Industries, Inc.

W. Howard Willey, Jr...........The Newburger Company

Julian C. Wilson...Attorney

Louis E. Wittenberg.........National Bank of Commerce

J. Will Young ....United Tennessee

Bancshares Corporation

CORPORATE MANAGEMENT

NATIONAL COMMERCE BANCORPORATION
BOARD OF DIRECTORS

Frank G. Barton, Jr. ....Barton Equipment Company

Jack R. Blair ....Smith & Nephew
Surgical Products Group

R. Grattan Brown, Jr. ....Glankler, Brown, Gilliland,
Chase, Robinson & Raines, Attorneys at Law

Bruce E. Campbell, Jr. .... National Commerce
Bancorporation and National Bank of Commerce

John D. Canale, III ....D. Canale Food Services, Inc.

Edmond D. Cicala................Edmond Enterprises, Inc.

James K. Dobbs, III ......Dobbs Brothers Management

John S. Evans...................National Bank of Commerce

Thomas C. Farnsworth, Jr. ....Real Estate
and Investments

Thomas M. Garrott.......................National Commerce
Bancorporation and National Bank of Commerce

R. Lee Jenkins ....formerly of Schering-Plough
Corporation and Plough, Inc.

Michael McDonnell................West Union Corporation

James E. McGehee, Jr..................McGehee Realty and
Development Company

W. Neely Mallory, Jr....................Memphis Compress &
Storage Company

Harry J. Phillips, Sr......Browning-Ferris Industries, Inc.

Rudi E. Scheidt..formerly of
Hohenberg Bros.Company

Robert M. Solmson ....RFS, Inc.

Sidney A. Stewart, Jr.....formerly of Sedgwick James, Inc.

R. Lee Taylor ....Private Investor

DIRECTORS EMERITUS

Walter P. Armstrong, Jr.; Lucius E. Burch, Jr.; John D. Canale, Jr.; E.J. Goldsmith, Jr.; Paul T. Graves; Thomas M. Keesee; John S. Montedonico; Joseph V. Montedonico, Jr.; Max B. Ostner, Sr.; and Robert G. Snowden

NATIONAL BANK OF COMMERCE
BOARD OF DIRECTORS

Frank G. Barton, Jr. ....Barton Equipment Company

Jack R. Blair.......................................Smith & Nephew
Surgical Products Group

R. Grattan Brown, Jr. ....Glankler, Brown,Gilliland,
Chase, Robinson & Raines, Attorneys at Law

Bruce E. Campbell, Jr...................National Commerce
Bancorporation and National Bank of Commerce

John D. Canale, III ....D. Canale Food Services, Inc.

Edmond D. Cicala................Edmond Enterprises, Inc.

James K. Dobbs, III ......Dobbs Brothers Management

John S. Evans...................National Bank of Commerce

Thomas C. Farnsworth, Jr......Real Estate and Investments

Thomas M. Garrott.......................National Commerce
Bancorporation and National Bank of Commerce

Walter B. Howell, Jr.........National Bank of Commerce

R. Lee Jenkins..................formerly of Schering-Plough
Corporation and Plough, Inc.

Michael McDonnell................West Union Corporation

James E. McGehee, Jr..................McGehee Realty and
Development Company

W. Neely Mallory, Jr...................Memphis Compress &
Storage Company

Harry J. Phillips, Sr.....Browning-Ferris Industries, Inc.

William R. Reed, Jr..........National Bank of Commerce

Rudi E. Scheidt..formerly of
Hohenberg Bros.Company

Robert M. Solmson..RFS, Inc.

Sidney A. Stewart, Jr....formerly of Sedgwick James, Inc.

R. Lee Taylor ....Private Investor

NATIONAL BANK OF COMMERCE
MANAGEMENT COMMITTEE

Bruce E. Campbell, Jr. ....Chairman of the Board
and Chief Executive Officer

Thomas M. Garrott ....President
and Chief Operating Officer

John S. Evans.......................................Vice Chairman
and Senior Loan Officer

Walter B. Howell, Jr. ....Vice Chairman
and Chief Financial Officer

William R. Reed, Jr. ....Vice Chairman

Gus B. Denton.......................Executive Vice President

Gary L. Lazarini....................Executive Vice President

Mackie H. Gober ....Executive Vice President

E. Walker Mulherin.....................Senior Vice President

Douglas W. Ferris, Jr. ....Senior Vice President

Hallam Boyd, Jr. ....Senior Vice President
and Senior Trust Officer

ACKNOWLEDGEMENTS

A FEW WORDS OF THANKS
FROM THE AUTHOR

Few authors ever produce substantive books without incurring obligations to others. Historians, since they can write only from information available on their subjects, especially require assistance from those who can provide the necessary records and explanations of factual material. Because the subject of this book was sometimes complicated and highly technical in some aspects, and because it extended across more than a century of change and progress, I have often found it necessary to seek the aid of others. Many people have generously given assistance and support. At the risk of overlooking some deserving individuals, I would like to give proper credit to those who have been most helpful to me.

Many of the events in the history of National Bank of Commerce during the 20th century cannot be fully understood on the basis of the written records alone. It has therefore been necessary to supplement the existing records with oral history interviews. These have taken the form of recollections and thoughtful explanations by persons who were astute observers of the bank during parts of its history from the decade of the 1920s to the present. Some of them were also leading participants in the development of the institution. They have taken time without reservation to share their knowledge with me. I am greatly indebted to them. They are: Walter P. Armstrong, Jr., Benjamin Goodman, John D. Canale, Jr., Lucius E. Burch, Jr., Robert G. Snowden, W. Neely Mallory, Jr., Rudi E. Scheidt, Wayne W. Pyeatt, Bruce E. Campbell, Jr., and Thomas M. Garrott.

A history of National Bank of Commerce requires considerable archival and illustrative material, both about the institution and its city, for the history of the bank has always been closely connected to that of the area it has served. Special thanks are due to many unknown past employees who believed that the various scrapbooks, financial records, clippings, and illus-trations they preserved would eventually be of importance. The bank records are fragmentary and incomplete, especially for the early years, but enough of them have been saved to enable an historian to piece together a coherent account of the internal operations of the institution. These records, having accompanied the bank during its moves from one location to another, are in reasonably good condition today.

The historical collection of the bank was supplemented by additional material. James R. Johnson and Patricia LaPointe of the Memphis & Shelby County Public Library gave much appreciated assistance in locating historical photographs and other material vital to this study. Michele L. Fagan, head of the Special Collections Department of the John Willard Brister Library at Memphis State University, was equally helpful. Competent and absolutely reliable research assistance in locating elusive source material was provided by Yvonne Phillips and Ann Meeks. Their faithful aid is much appreciated. Most newspapers published in Memphis during the past 120 years were searched for information, but particular credit must be given to *The Commercial Appeal* and its various predecessors. This is appropriate, since the founders of this newspaper in its present form were mainly individuals associated with the original Bank of Commerce.

No author could have received more diligent and courteous support from the staff of any financial institution than I was given by the directors, officers, and employees of National Bank of Commerce. Support of my work was a team effort on the part of many of them, but I wish to express thanks specifically to several who were most helpful to me. Charles A. Neale, vice president and general counsel, has demonstrated the ability to explain intricate legal and organizational arrangements in a manner that a layman can understand. He has also made useful suggestions about the improvement of the text. Walter B. Howell, Jr., vice chairman and chief financial officer, has provided financial information and interpreted it in language comprehensible to an historian. William L. Richmond, senior vice president, trust division, who was a bank officer when Robert Talley's history was written 40 years ago, has enlightened this author with some of the unwritten history of the firm.

When an author writes a book, his family and friends are affected by any sacrifices and difficulties he experiences. Mine have patiently endured many months during which my attention was largely in another world — that of the subject about which I was writing during its different eras. Understanding the truth of the saying, "Lincoln freed all the slaves — except authors," they have been aware of the months of labor required by this study. Much of the writing of the book has been done between the hours of sunset and sunrise, and during this time I have found it necessary to develop the habits of a recluse. I hope my family and friends find the enjoyment of reading this volume worth the time I had to spend away from them in the other world of writing.

Betty H. Williams, of the Oral History Research Office of Memphis State University, has uncomplainingly accepted my irregular attention span while the manuscript was in preparation. My students during

this time have probably observed that my perspective has inclined more than usual toward institutional and economic aspects of history.

Three members of the National Bank of Commerce family deserve a special expression of gratitude for their unique contributions to the book. Director Emeritus Lucius E. Burch, Jr., a friend of many years, whose companionship I have enjoyed during memorable hunting experiences in field and forest, and while philosophizing by blazing fires in the evenings, has honored me as well as the bank by his willingness to write the introduction to the book. M. J. "Jekka" Ashman, vice president of deposit services, has served as general editor during the entire writing and production of this history. Her remarkable ability, like that of the other young officers of the bank, gives hope that its future will be as successful as its past. Her skill as an editor as well as a banker has my respect and appreciation. Bruce E. Campbell, Jr., chief executive officer and chairman of the board of National Bank of Commerce, has led the institution through its greatest era of growth and prosperity. In ancient times, a leader of such conspicuous success might have left a statue of himself as his legacy to the future. In the Renaissance Era, a merchant prince would likely have commissioned a painting, also of himself. In the modern age, a business magnate directing a corporation with assets of billions of dollars might have arranged for the publication of a biography. Bruce Campbell instead decided to leave a history, and hopefully an accurate and professionally written one, of the bank he has led, loved, and served. I hope this book endures for at least 120 more years as a memorial to his effective leadership and unselfish devotion to his bank.

Last, but of surpassing importance, I am indebted to Carlie Elizabeth Crawford, my mother, who by her hard work, thrift, and investment in my future, taught me the basic and still true things I know about finance. And, most of all, she taught me about the things that cannot be bought with money.

Charles W. Crawford

CREDITS

SPECIAL THANKS TO THE FOLLOWING FOR THEIR GENEROUS CONTRIBUTIONS OF PHOTOGRAPHS AND EXHIBITS:

Page 108 ....National Bank of Commerce

Page 113 ....National Bank of Commerce

Page 118 ....National Bank of Commerce

Page 120 ....National Bank of Commerce

Page 121 ....National Bank of Commerce

Page 122 ....National Bank of Commerce

On the dustjacket:

Passbooks, circa 1874 and 1893..............Gus B. Denton

Book-shaped bank with key, circa 1927........................

National Bank of Commerce

Picture postcards, circa 1906 and 1920.....Gus B. Denton

Other photos....................National Bank of Commerce